The Long Devotion

POETS

The Long

WRITING

Devotion

MOTHERHOOD

EDITED BY **Emily Pérez**

AND **Nancy Reddy**

THE UNIVERSITY OF
GEORGIA PRESS
ATHENS

© 2022 by the University of Georgia Press
Athens, Georgia 30602
www.ugapress.org
All rights reserved
Designed by Kaelin Chappell Broaddus
Set in 10/14 Dolly Pro Regular by Kaelin Chappell Broaddus
Printed and bound by TK
The paper in this book meets the guidelines for permanence and durability of the Committee on Production Guidelines for Book Longevity of the Council on Library Resources.

Published with the generous support of the Sustainable Arts Foundation and Tony and Caroline Grant.

Most University of Georgia Press titles are available from popular e-book vendors.

Printed in the United States of America
25 24 23 22 21 P 5 4 3 2 1

Library of Congress Cataloging-in-Publication Data in Process

ISBN: 9780820360546 (pbk.: alk. paper)
ISBN: 9780820360584 (ebook)

Contents

Foreword: How It Feels

Because I believe in radical honesty, I will let you know that I put the editors of the book you hold in your hands through a great deal of strain.

The problem was, they couldn't be sure, until practically the last moment, whether or not I could be counted on to write the foreword I had promised to write.

I am sorry, Emily. Please understand, Nancy. These are difficult times.

The world we live in too often devalues the work of mothers. Anyone with this book in their hands, I suspect, already trusts that last sentence is true. But, sometimes, mothers and their children are lifted up. Which is the main thing—thank you, thank you—that the poems, prompts, and essays in this anthology do.

Emily, dear Emily, sent me a kind query nearly every month, month after month, over a period of roughly ten months. Her emails contained updates about the progress of this anthology, where things stood with the contents, where things stood with the press. It was as if I were receiving updates on this baby's development, complete with reports from doctor visits and images from 3D ultrasounds. I got glimpses of the book before it was birthed into the world!

In each email, Emily was excited and a little wary. I'd promised to do my part to help this precious entity as it developed, but could she count on me? Would anyone else be as excited about this book as the women whose labor brought it to life?

The truth is, they had reason to doubt. I have been preoccupied with my own family, my own writing, my own life. Haven't we all?

It took me a long time to sit down with the anthology—this collection of ultrasounds. But the day I finally did, that is all that I did. I didn't get up from my reading chair for hours. I was absolutely and completely captivated, as I trust you will be too.

To risk pushing this metaphor all the way to the end, it was as if I'd finally slowed down long enough to hold a friend's baby.

Maybe I was a bit jealous my friend's circumstances allowed her to have a child—I've experienced this kind of despairing frustration before, have you? Or maybe I was just very very busy, like I already said I was busy, and I hadn't figured out a way to make time for some other humans' newly created life—we all get busy, right? These are unprecedented times. We have so much to do.

But I am here now, the child in my arms, and the world has slowed, and my breath has slowed, and my connection to things beyond me is clearer than it has been for a very long time.

I am glad for this chance to connect with something, with someone, vulnerable and compact and brilliant in a manner that runs deeper than words. Page after page, offering after offering, that is how it feels to sit with this book. Like being gentled long enough to hold a newborn baby. Like feeling whole and seen and wild and grateful and raw and scarred and honest and open and connected again.

Reading this book feels like that. Startling and awesome. Like how it feels to hold a new beginning and to know you can hold that beginning again and again and again.

CAMILLE T. DUNGY
Written July 2020, in the
early hours while my own
growing child still sleeps

Introduction

This book emerged from a shared question: what does it mean to be a mother who writes? Both writing and raising children require time, energy, and attention. If you add working to this list—whether in or outside the home—resources become even tighter. We wondered, did writing and mothering have to be in competition, or were there ways the two could inspire and feed one another?

Before we had our own children, before we began writing while mothering, we'd heard years of cautionary tales about the havoc children would wreak on a life of art. The whispered stories went like this: Babies would steal your time, your intellect, your ambition. You'd stop writing, or if you kept it up somehow, your poems would all turn to sentimental goo. These worries were shaped by the tradition we still, in the early twenty-first century, live and write from, one that's rooted in patriarchy, one in which motherhood and children have been seen as necessarily sentimental subjects. We'd been taught that "sentiment" is the enemy of "quality," that any writing taking up these subjects could be summarily dismissed as unrelatable to a wider reading audience, or as too niche to be "serious" writing. We both feared writing what Joy Katz, one of our contributors, has called "the bad poem with a baby in it."

And yet, other experiences that are not shared by all people have been treated as vital to our understanding of humankind. As poet Sasha West reasons in the essay included in this book, "War Songs: Mothering through Climate Change," "No one questioned the way war could be a lens. Though the writers were unlike me—mostly male, elsewhere in history and geography—both my teachers and I understood there to be value in experiences that move your body into a different kind of knowing. It was the strangeness of the lives we didn't share that widened our own. No one expected war poems to be universal or relatable. (We hoped they wouldn't be.) What was valuable was how they let us see what happens at the edges of humanity." West continues to liken the strangeness of war, the way it takes the body to "a different kind of knowing," to motherhood. Motherhood has so much to teach about the human condition.

Once we started looking, we found many mothers taking up that charge. The writing world was full of people managing somehow to write *and* mother, and often to combine those activities in really interesting ways. Some of the writers we knew rose early or stayed up late, writing while their children slept. Some left home to go on writing residencies (often ad hoc stays in hotels or friends' homes, since many of the prestigious residencies require stays of two weeks or more that are difficult for parents of young children to manage). And some simply wrote through their children's disruptions, allowing their children's voices and bodies and demands to enter the writing. We set out in this book to learn both what mothers were writing and also how they were getting that writing done.

In this book, we've gathered a wide range of voices and approaches. We've included poems that show the joy of experiencing the world through children's eyes alongside poems that show the immense challenges of raising children. Our contributors include stepparents, adoptive and foster parents, those struggling with infertility, and those who've chosen to remain childless. The writing in this book chronicles postpartum depression, parenting a child with autism, making space for writing while struggling with chronic illness and mental health challenges, and the intensely bodily joys and heartaches of pregnancy, birth, and parenting. These poems and essays present a diverse, frank, and richly varied range of perspectives on motherhood. Together, this writing aims to celebrate motherhood and also create a space for mothers to, as poet Molly Spencer has written, "tell an unlovely truth about family life and not have to take it back."

This book consists of four parts, and each part includes poems, essays, and writing prompts. "Difficulty, Ambivalence, and Joy" takes on motherhood broadly. It includes expressions of ambivalence about having children and poems on infertility, abortion, and miscarriage alongside poems that celebrate pregnancy, birth, and motherhood. "The Body and the Brain" examines the relationship between the bodily work of motherhood and the cerebral work of writing, as well as how illness or chronic conditions impact the work of both mothering and writing. "In the World" considers how motherhood brings people into contact with spaces outside the home—from the neighborhood to global politics, from cross-cultural exchange to racialized violence, from war to wonder at the natural landscape. Finally, "Transitions" looks at how mothering and writing change over time, particularly as children begin to grow up.

During the years we crafted this book, motherhood entered public conversations in a big way. Across the political spectrum, conversations about the necessity of support for working families such as paid family leave and affordable, high-quality childcare seem to have finally gained traction. Celebrities spoke on Twitter and the covers of magazines about a host of formerly taboo topics like infertility, in vitro fertilization, miscarriage, and postpartum depression. And, as the book took shape, our own lives as mothers evolved, and we scheduled calls around our kids' playdates, naps, crises, and homework. Sometimes we typed and talked with children sitting on our laps and sometimes we kept working while ignoring our children yelling in some other part of the house. And in the final months we spent on the book, our families experienced a whole new level of togetherness and stress as the social distancing and "shelter in place" orders brought on by the coronavirus meant we were mostly confined to our homes.

This book has been the work of years: a truly countless number of emails and phone calls and text messages to set up phone calls and requests for just a couple more minutes while we sent our kids out to play or got them set up with a game or TV show. During the crafting of this book, Nancy's older son started elementary school and learned to read. Her younger son enrolled in the district pre-K and began to write his name and draw long-limbed stick figures he taped to the wall in her office. Emily's kids moved toward mid– and late–elementary school, struggling with and adapting to diagnoses of ADHD, dyslexia, and depression. They also learned to do front flips on a trampoline, typed stories about wolves and farting shopping carts, became interested in politics, and composed original music for piano. The work of editing this collection has also been the work of writing/motherhood: fragmented, and alternately enriched and challenged by the work of caring for our children.

We read widely, finding poems we adored that helped us think about motherhood in all kinds of new ways. We wrote to poets whose work inspired us and asked them to become part of this book, and we asked many of them to write essays about their own path through writing and motherhood.

This book has been a journey that has deepened our own understanding of the many ways that writing and motherhood inform each other. We hope you will take up this journey with us through reading, sharing this work with others, and writing your own poems.

Difficulty, Ambivalence, and Joy

IN PARENTING, JOY AND DIFFICULTY ARE INEXTRICABLY linked. Although our culture often expects mothers to express unmitigated joy (and even a sense of duty) at the prospect of a baby, the path there can be complicated. Whether a child arrives via birth or adoption; whether the baby is planned, unplanned, or conceived via fertility treatments; whether pregnancy and birth are easy or draining; whether a pregnancy ends in miscarriage or abortion or never happens at all, contemplating and perhaps choosing motherhood is often more fraught than sitcoms or Hallmark cards would have it.

The poems in this part explore the powerful emotions—anxiety, euphoria, depression, and even rage—that accompany the work of mothering. It opens with a poem that considers the intense confluence of difficulty, ambivalence, and joy: in Catherine Pierce's "High Dangerous," the speaker juxtaposes her children's glee at spotting hydrangeas and their fear of the bees that buzz around the flowers with the terrors of the world they don't yet recognize and her desire to protect them from that knowledge. Then, the poems move from early pregnancy, as in Heid E. Erdrich's "Intimate Detail," to babyhood, as in Carrie Fountain's "To White Noise," and into the tween and teen years with Carmen Giménez Smith's "Rare Privilege." Many poems explore how love for one's child can be intimately coupled with exhaustion and frustration. Emily Mohn-Slate's "Feed," for example, demonstrates the sometimes overwhelming work of caring for a newborn.

These poems also examine some of the difficulties of mothering itself, beginning with the choice to become a mother and the many ways that family is made. In "Confession," Kiki Petrosino speaks to the child she's considering having, the one she chooses, month after month, *not* to conceive. Keetje Kuipers celebrates the modern technology that made her a single mother by choice through in vitro fertilization in "The Museum of Trades and Traditions." Megan Snyder-Camp, a foster mother and biological mother, considers what those identities mean for herself, her family, and the mothers of the children she fosters in "Permanency." In Remica Bingham-Risher's "We See *The Lion King* on Broadway, I Enter the Pride," a blended family shares a special occasion, after which the stepmother speaker of the poem notes that "everything the light touches is ours." Even in the midst of ordinary and extraordinary challenges in motherhood, these writers also manage to find joy and transcendence.

The essays in this part consider the difficulties inherent in sustaining a creative life while performing the joyful and demanding work of mothering. In "Mothering Solo," Khadijah Queen describes how she's worked to make space for her writing as a single mother, and her assertion that "Being a mother often makes the act of writing even more urgent, more sanity-saving, more necessary" is one that rings true for many mothers, regardless of the particulars of their family life. Megan Snyder-Camp's "Baskets" considers how, as a foster mother, she can write ethically about the children whose place in her family is temporary. Her contemplation of the ethics of writing about children who can't yet fully speak for themselves is a valuable one for all writers.

We've found reading and writing about mothering—the beauty and the hardship, and everything else along the way—to be a vital tool in our own motherhood journeys.

High Dangerous

CATHERINE PIERCE

is what my sons call the flowers—
purple, white, electric blue—

pom-pomming bushes all along
the beach town streets.

I can't correct them into
hydrangeas, or I won't.

Bees ricochet in and out
of the clustered petals,

and my sons panic and dash
and I tell them about good

insects, pollination, but the truth is
I want their fear-box full of bees.

This morning the radio
said *tender age shelters*.

This morning the glaciers
are retreating. How long now

until the space-print backpack
becomes district-policy clear?

We're almost to the beach,
and *High dangerous!* my sons

yell again, their joy in having
spotted something beautiful,

and called it what it is.

Intimate Detail

HEID E. ERDRICH

Late summer, late afternoon, my work
interrupted by bees who claim my tea,
even my pen looks flower-good to them.
I warn a delivery man that my bees,
who all summer have been tame as cows,
now grow frantic, aggressive, difficult to shoo
from the house. I blame the second blooms
come out in hot colors, defiant vibrancy—
unexpected from cottage cosmos, nicotiana,
and bean vine. But those bees know, I'm told
by the interested delivery man, they have only
so many days to go. He sighs at sweetness untasted.

Still warm in the day, we inspect the bees.
This kind stranger knows them in intimate detail.
He can name the ones I think of as *shopping ladies.*
Their fur coats ruffed up, yellow packages tucked
beneath their wings, so weighted with their finds
they ascend in slow circles, sometimes drop, while
other bees whirl madly, dance the blossoms, ravish
broadly so the whole bed bends and bounces alive.

He asks if I have kids, I say not yet. He has five,
all boys. He calls the honeybees his girls although
he tells me they're *ungendered workers*
who never produce offspring. Some hour drops,
the bees shut off. In the long, cool slant of sun,
spent flowers fold into cups. He asks me if I've ever
seen a *Solitary Bee* where it sleeps. I say I've not.
The nearest bud's a long-throated peach hollyhock.
He cradles it in his palm, holds it up so I spy
the intimacy of the sleeping bee. Little life safe in a petal,
little girl, your few furious buzzings as you stir
stay with me all winter, remind me of my work undone.

The Monarch

SHARA LESSLEY

Once, I was decorative, could
stand very still, quiet as a thumb-
tack holding up what was important.
I was handsome, too, in the right
weather, my heart like a pool of
metallic shavings, or the thoughtless
whirr of a curtain catching whatever
the pane let in. Is it true we worship
things made in our likeness? My face
in my daughter's face, sharp as time's
punch line: that she carries the youth
that was mine. I watch myself
walking the long blocks from fall
to spring, the schoolboys in filed
companies ignoring even my shadow.
Vanity's a funny thing. The shelves
all lined with ointments and creams;
my mirror, like a hunter's camera
set on a carcass, trying to game
the game. In captivity, elephants
have been known to grind their
tusks against the walls of their cells,
nights passed upright and swaying
as if to lull themselves away from sleep
rather than toward it. I understand
their defeat. As if happiness were a button
lost in the grass, not the protractor's
dance on a graph as we try to connect
our lives' little squares. For years
I mistook the Polaroid of my mother
holding me in the car as our first
together, but here we are among the wild
asparagus, high as bamboo, as though
no labor could break her. In the photo,
she commands a rake, while I wait, six

weeks to go in utero, my retinas
pulsing toward scraps of light.
My second pregnancy took years
off my life. Bedridden and hooked
to tubes, I worried my daughter
wouldn't outlive the darkness of
the womb, her brain shedding any
synapse related to sight. In this photo,
all is fine—my father watching over
my mother's shoulder beneath a sky
too blue to be true, which has something
to do with why, when my daughter
begins to cry, having discovered—
after coaxing it from its pupa—
the withered butterfly, I call its death
a trick of light. In her sketchbook,
we trace the proboscis, the compound eye
that would have tracked the sun's
descent. We label the antennae,
the wings' delicate panes. The monarch
wanted back its cocoon, I explain,
because the light was too much.
She fiddles with an orange crayon.
I push the mesh cage aside; meaning,
I do what my mother did. Pretending
abandonment is natural, I smile. And lie.

Confession

KIKI PETROSINO

Every month I decide not to try
is a lungful of gold I can keep for myself.
Still, I worry you'll come to me anyhow

& hitch your hiccuping bud. My dear
I don't want to be got. I just want to get done
with this month. I decide not to try.

I decide on a wine. You keep spinning
through the woods on green stars of pollen.
Still, I worry you'll come to me anyhow.

Your small breath troubles the flour
I'm spilling. Did you leave sweet jam on the sill?
Every month, I decide not to try

to find out. Late sun butters the glitz
in my guts. My dear, I'm already botched.
Still, I worry you'll come to me anyhow.

Lately, I've dreamed of quilts stuffed
with bees; it's a thing. Yet I don't see
why I worry & worry. You come to me anyhow
every month I decide not to try.

At the Museum of Trades and Traditions

KEETJE KUIPERS

Here is the tool with the delicate
handle designated to turn a tree trunk

into a pipe for channeling water. And here
is the tortoise shell carved into combs

of paisley gold. Here are the tin stamps
once pressed into warm butter to raise

the outline of milkmaid or sunrise
on its hardening surface. Here the tobacco horns,

here the looms, here the little knives
and the elegant silver-plated pistols. We say,

Which job would you have picked?
Butter churner or glassblower? Blacksmith

or weaver? Though, as women, we wouldn't
have had so many options. Unlike my daughter,

whose father I chose from a list of hair
and eye color, narrowing the field by height

and weight and college major. Someday I'll find
that tool in a museum, the squat centrifuge,

the gasping seal of its lid, the gentle click
and whir as it swirled the sperm into a thin serum.

Or perhaps the slight catheter designed
to angle past the cervix and into the ether

of my womb. There, on velvet, under a soft light
in some airless case, the tools that made me a mother.

The Leopard

JOY LADIN

for Yael

You are reporting on the leopard. You are only seven
and you already know the leopard
comes in greys as well as yellows.

The leopard's children
tumble in the shadow of a rock.
Gazelle bolt in the distance.

Reporting on the leopard
turns life and death
into simple declarative sentences.

The gazelle ignores the leopard
until the leopard snaps its neck.
In your kitchen love and hate

shadow each other
the way you are shadowed
by the birthday that tiptoes closer.

You are only seven and you already know
you are the prey
of the love you cannot escape. Love

flings its kill over branches
in the jungle
that is your kitchen.

You are only seven and you already know
its spots will make love hard to see
until it snaps your neck.

Sestina Gratitude

JOYELLE MCSWEENEY

Thank you in gold particle. Thank you in wave. Thank you any zygote worth its salt.
Bend down to be capacitated. Bend down to take your crown. Thank you
parting membrane. Thank you for the crown
that wants to be a noose. Thank you—slip down,
cervical vertebrae. Thank you, fontanel. You have turned this brain
into a fosse. Thank you scouts

spreading out across the grain. Your doggy snouts
now pick up the scent of blood. Thank you thought, that salty
tinsel ribboning the hundred dollar bill. Thank you, rib bone. The brain
mints double currency, twin waves at twin across a river, you
my brother and you, my veiny border. For you I roll my syndrome down
to zero. I stop the clock; a stopped clock's a double crown

and it says zero zero, while the crowd
shouts from the bleachers, bleached of stain, shouts
shalts and shalt nots while the ball crests, sinks down
to fill the basket like a crown, upside down. Water and salt
fill the isolation tank where this moment is suspended, you
and your brain rock there, sapless as a brain

-dead babe. Sadcoat, trenchcoat, dressed for war, a drain
to drain the wound and a drain fitted to the heart, crowded
with gold husks, principles, fixtures, faults, bacteria, you
golden hand that melts the bone, shout
at the bullet smelter, two lungs hung-up in the steeple, salt
lantern blown out corrosive, smearing the sea with blonde down.

Down comes the beam, it decays and sheds, it lays a lacquer down
under the golden dome, the brain in its jacket
shines and shines and lies down in the salt marsh
down in the kennel with the hunting dogs, crowded with breath,
and accommodates a gold bullet in both hemispheres, the bullet shouts
thought's steeple down. You

lie down like a river as thought spills out on straw. You
are the liquor that steams down
the seam of the jeans. You the suture stemmed with gold, stout
rivets, miner's hammer, you the hammer to the brain,
you the footfall of the scouts, shouts in the thicket, you the crowd
that waves its tickets, blonde train smeared with light, trail of salt

which marks the battledress like a wingbeat drawn on serge. You
the surge, the shout. You the battledead, the widow's salt, the bullet
in the crown. You the salted aquifer. The pulseless fontanel.

Self-Portrait as God with a Stillborn Inside

CHELSEA DINGMAN

Here is the room that made you a saint.

Here is the well. Your body, soon excavated
from mine. A little voice, not yours. Not divine—

here is the mother I might've been. The months

of preparation. The end of times. An era of false
imprisonment. My water will break & flood you

out. I'll wait for a sigh. The soft smack of your skull

on bloody thighs. This captivity is my fault. I want
to keep you longer. *Let there be light.* There is no bucket,

no rope. This isn't a nursery rhyme. *Let the earth bring forth*

living creatures after their kind. I have given warmth
& water to the earth. The plants & birds. The dry

seed of you trapped inside me. I have multiplied.

I have given everything to liken myself to the rime.
Beware of the body-lie. Body-quiet. The spirit

body. Believe me: childbirth is war. Let the blade

learn you. Let your throat soften against it.
Let the rules of war not apply. Here, creation

theory ends with thrashing. A drowning.

A body pulled from the dark & soldered
to the sky. This morning I made: keep it.

Only one of us is lying. I'll be just fine.

Postpartum: Lullaby

CHELSEA RATHBURN

When two-thirty midnight ten
When the baby cries again

When at her breast a parasite
When she is up and down all night

A voice like a wound in her head in her ear
A rational wound calm and clear

By day she whispers promises
By day she smiles and swaddles and kisses

By night beneath a callous moon
When she alone can soothe she croons

aloud aloud the unallowed
I want to blow my brains out now

And still they rock and rock and rock
beside a cold indifferent clock

Feed

EMILY MOHN-SLATE

Wind whips the umbrella on the porch like a ship's sail
I watch it twist   and lean over the counter eating   numb-eyed

The baby rolls in the monitor's blue fuzz
and I calculate how long until he needs to eat again

I've been going for months   If I stop, I will be ordinary
All I want to do is feed myself bread and milk

I cut the baby out of the poem
I put the baby back in

The geese are migrating somewhere
One lags behind   veering

unsatisfied by its pocket in the V
the group's squawking mind to move

maybe hating those beating bodies ahead
I need the baby to take a nap   I need the baby to not need me

I never meant to be so needed
I dream about drifting   alone
I can't quiet my ambition
It bats at my knees and I toss it scraps

hoping it will reward me for wrenching off each finger
each thick arm   my teeming head

dropping them   one by one   into the black well of its jaws

To White Noise

CARRIE FOUNTAIN

You are the sound silence
makes in its sleep, air made

visible by smoke, deepest
breath with no breathing,

O my personal ocean, O unbroken shush of mortality,

O my digital sister, thank
you, thank you for keeping

the children from climbing
over the fence of sleep.

We See *The Lion King* on Broadway, I Enter the Pride

REMICA BINGHAM-RISHER

Our girl is telling the boys to pose near the theater doors.
We have traveled to the Minskoff in New York

and the children are finally elated.
They have been trying to teach me

their ways—they wrestle and weary one another,
bending and binding love—but I am useless in my tenderness

until this: I have orchestrated the daytrip of dreams.
Herald Square gleams like a lost enchantress.

As we scuttle and preen, she tries pashminas and caps,
designer shades, everything neon at once. When our tickets have been taken

and they step into the circle, for a flash of moment,
she takes the journey in. It is only a measure

before the music starts, while we head to our seats,
she says   *This is amazing—*

all you've done to get us here. It must have taken
hours. Years, I think, years, but she is grateful

and I am finally useful. As the curtain goes up,
everything the light touches is ours.

Permanency

MEGAN SNYDER-CAMP

My son loves microscopic water bears because they need nothing
have nothing and are everywhere. Not parasites just everywhere.

Honey when I die I will be in all of this too, Play-Doh
stretched to lace, furnace filter thickened with our skin cells.

If I'm everywhere will I get closer to nothing, if I claim
less and less of myself, leave it spinning on the carousel.

The new girl in our family calls me mama
and my daughter tells her no. Well but I am the mama of this house.

I am the furnace filter keeping you safe and warm.
The girl has had so many mamas that at her birthday party

some of us stand in the hall. She wants up
so we pass her from arm to arm, tree to tree. Her mother

is one of us. Her mother is not one of us.
Her mother does not say a word

when my son tells the story of the immortal jellyfish
who crumple down into babies again and again, unlike water bears

who can have no water for a hundred years but are always fine.

I'm Your Mom

LAUREN HALDEMAN

I am your Mom. You don't have to test your
hold — you can use the vines, you can pull
yourself up

by my teeth.

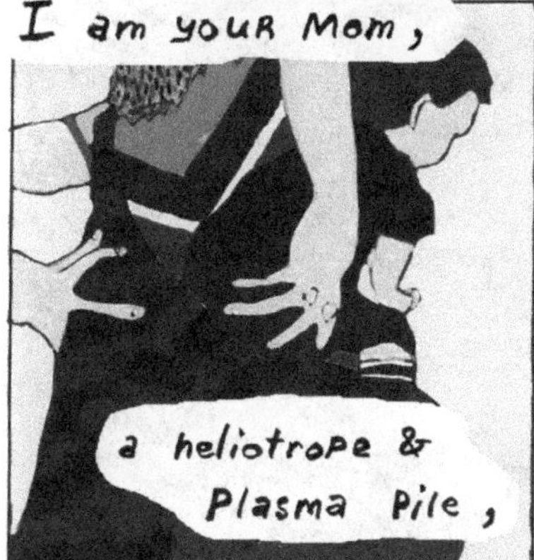
I am your Mom,
a heliotrope &
Plasma Pile,

steady,
weather passing me;

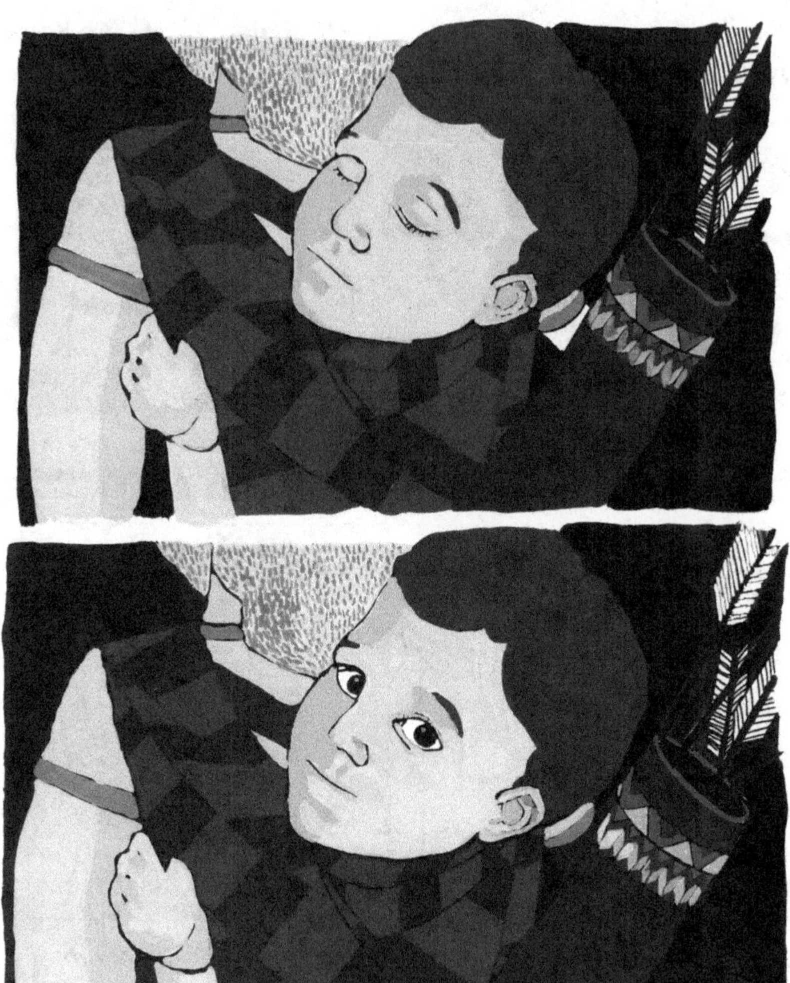

this is my job, I'm your Mom,

I am astronaut, helmeted raven; I am neutrons, plum-pits, core-mantle metallurgy.

Dear P.

VICTORIA CHANG

Please forage please do not achieve please

stay mischievous even if others are deviously

perfect your previous hair color will always be black

black isn't absence black shouldn't be auctioned

black has options even if you have to hack something

rip something lengthwise your soul isn't a

flagpole it can lift up into the sky and wave

become frayed you too can have but make

sure you actually want otherwise stay home

and make your own wontons they won't get

stuck to your tonsils someday someone will seal you

out but someday someone will also sing to you

from a windowsill and steal you from me

because you were never only mine

Landscape with Clinic and Oracle

LYNN MELNICK

Maybe you're not the featherweight champ
of all the cutthroat combat sports

(fifteen and pregnant
again)

but you'd convert your ring corner
into a slaughterhouse

before you'd inquire after human kindness.

In the humdrum flare outside the clinic
you wait for a ride, feel the spill at the tipping point

trickle down your inner thigh
as you bask in the post-industrial particulate

on your skin, ash
into a jasmine pot's bituminous anchorage

so tacky it glows in a habitat that spent your body
long before it finished growing.

  Lynn! they lied to you

don't you know?
Your womb will be the first thing to heal.

What you smell is pleasure, not the rot of the thing
amid the waste.

You will have babies.
You will write poems about flowers that turn on in darkness.

Virgil, Hey

CAMILLE GUTHRIE

Ah me! I find myself middle-aged divorced lost
In the forest dark of my failures mortgage & slack breasts
It's hard to admit nobody wants to do me anymore
Not even Virgil will lead me down to his basement rental

Take a look at my firstborn son
Who put me on three months' bedrest
For whom I bled on the emergency room floor
Who declaims his device sucks
Stabs holes in his bedroom wall
Complains his ATV's too slow
Who plots to run away to join terrorists
He'd rather die than do math

And the little one ripped
From my womb in the surgery room
I pierced my nipples to unblock her milk
Who pours lemonade on the floor for skating
Howls in rage cause her cake isn't pretty
Carved "No Mom" on her door with scissors
Who says, "No fence but you're kinda fat"
She'd rather die than wear underpants

Virgil, hey! Send me down
To the second circle of hell where I belong
With those whom Love separated from Reason
Where an infernal hurricane will blast me
Hither & thither with no hope ever no comfort
Rather than drive these two to school this morning
And suffer forever with the other mothers

Rare Privilege

CARMEN GIMÉNEZ SMITH

What my children do not know fills volumes.
It's the least I could do. Sometimes I want
to crack their illusions open because they are
the illusions of the carefree, therefore
the concerns of the children I hated
when I was bucktoothed and hungry for class,
but I am not cruel. My worst infractions
are raising my voice, and working
through and thus over their childhood
because that's what being a mother
was. If all goes as planned, when they
undo the ribbon on the Pandora box of
adulthood, they'll only see smiles and low
interest rates. That's what I came here to do.
I still can't wait to hear about their failures,
though. I'll lean in to their face and eat
every word as if they were my last breaths.

Mothering Solo

KHADIJAH QUEEN

Mothering is the ultimate convergence of public and private. From the moment your belly swells, the fact that you are/have been sexually active becomes publicly displayed. The implicit questions: *Who has impregnated you? Does he have cultural/institutional permission? Do you, expectant mother, have permission? Where is the piece of paper/(in)expensive ornament on your hand that says so?*

Then, assumptions begin—your body changes, and strangers act as witness. Sometimes, they want to touch you. You are full of life; you are sensitive, physically and emotionally. You are urgent in every way, and strangers, smiling, touch you, often without permission, ask you personal questions. You might feel okay about that, or you might be offended. The point is—vision. Outside, inside. How you see yourself in relation to others, how they see themselves in relation to you. We are all of us mirrors. We see what we want, we look for what we want or look for what we fear.

Is there some kind of human aversion to our own bodies that makes life-growing a shame to so many? That is what I would ask those who treat single mothers differently, consciously or unconsciously, no matter their age or economic status. Something deep is at work in the human psyche. I am hinting at the ugliest and most fundamental of truths, and single motherhood, I promise, is merely tangential.

Women who give birth out of wedlock or who have somehow separated from their partners have traditionally been shamed—for their aloneness, their state of supposed non-support, as if their vulnerability makes them difficult to look at, or worse, unworthy of being truly seen, because the damage—think of it! a child as damage, a child as shame—has been done. It's not often talked about in these PC days, but the shadow lingers—an Eliot-esque smoke along the windowpanes as we peer at one another in social situations. Soccer games, bake sales, PTA meetings, clothes shopping, dinner at Outback. The automatic glance at the ring finger. This is worth saying aloud: Our worth, our children's worth, is not tied to a masculine presence at the dinner table.

❧

Not that I don't feel the absence of a partner to help shoulder day-to-day responsibilities, especially the things I least enjoy doing, like bringing groceries in or maintaining the car. Some days I work so much and for so long that by the time the day ends, unsurprisingly, I feel numb from exhaustion. And I still have to make dinner, be patient, be loving, iron clothes, give instructions, wash dishes, host sleepovers, encourage—without germophobia—scientific experiments that take over the bathtub. Sometimes I fail, sometimes I am miraculously successful; sometimes I am resentful, sometimes I feel so lucky. Sometimes all of the above and more happen in the same day and I want to burst. But that's life. Would it be nice to have some help? Sure. Would I trade it to have a husband, for the sake of having a husband, and the financial and physical labor-easing such a union supposedly implies? Absolutely not. I'm not judging any married person or anyone else's choices, but I personally value my independence more than any supposed convenience.

❧

Which brings me to writing. We—mothers who write, solo mothers who write and create—often, if not most of the time or all of the time, write for our lives. Being a mother often makes the act of writing even more urgent, more sanity-saving, more necessary. We can get lost in routine and duty, obviously, but getting lost in the love part—love of our children, love of writing—might prevent that. Part of that is self-love. Part of that is creative output. All of it meant to keep us connected to who we are, as creative beings, when external forces might sever or corrupt such connection.

Parenting takes everything you have and more. Parenting solo—just like any kind of human activity—means nothing is perfect: you make mistakes, you run out of energy, you ultimately have only yourself to depend on. Sometimes things get done halfway. None of that fits into the obsessive perfectionism that strongly underlies current parenting norms. Thankfully, though, it fits with our basic humanness, which means we can forgive ourselves, and accept ourselves (and our children) as we are.

❧

The stigma attached to single mothers, frankly, baffles me. The most prevalent question I've gotten as a single mother: *How do you do it?* My answer: One thing (or two or seven) at a time, minute by minute, shoelace by shoelace, tantrum by tantrum, laugh by laugh, story by story. I order out; I cook a bunch on weekends; I pass out with my clothes on; I let some things slide, or stay up late to finish. We, as parents, repeat ourselves. And it's a good thing: we're teaching our children how to live. Thank goodness each day we get another chance at almost everything.

❧

This essay is clearly not an explanation of my situation, why I am single, or whether or not I chose to be. None of that matters. It matters that my son is alive with humor, that he is as fragile a human being as all of us, and that he has the strongest heart I know. It matters that he is brilliant and curious and incredibly kind. But, having tired of that kindness thrown back in his face, he will fight if he must. And as much as it hurts, I know he'll have to. His dark brown skin is the hunted kind; his thick hair and wide shoulders will only grow in perceived threat to some.

❧

The most important thing I have learned as a parent is to trust my child.

In trusting him, I learned, slowly, to trust myself. It spilled into my work. I wrote the way I wanted to, because it was fun, because it felt good, because it mattered, and it didn't have to make sense, because it only had to matter to me, at first. I could figure out the rest once the writing part was done.

❧

Mothering and working means that some things fall down the scale of importance; some fall off. Some return, some do not—they might flicker in the distance or disappear, even from memory. I don't even miss some of those things, and the others I've developed a resigned and optimistic appreciation of later.

When parsing time and energy, the now becomes everything: shelter, hunger, sleep, warmth. I pay attention; the consequence otherwise may cost unbearably more than if I don't. Because my son and I both have physical challenges, comfort for us becomes the scaffolding upon which the rest of our lives takes shape, even our emotional well-being.

Of hyper-importance: what we eat, where we go, how much rest I get. We've become connoisseurs of one another's moods, and our closeness tied to our health. My writing is tied to my health. I must write. I taught my son to respect and support that. He is older now, and able to understand. He knows I feel better (and that I am a better mother) when and because I nurture my creative work, and he loves that about me. And I support his obsession with incredibly complex strategy-oriented Japanese card games. I take him to tournaments and even play, sometimes, though poorly, when he really wants me to. We allow one another to be who we are. I am lucky. We enjoy our lives. We are a family.

Sunday Dinner

LISA L. MOORE

The queerest thing about our family is not that we are lesbians raising two cisgender boys. Or that the older boy told us at fifteen that he might be—"no, no, I AM"—bisexual. His younger brother, fifteen as I write, has not declared himself and makes it clear we are not to ask. The queerest thing is not the compulsory activism that puts them at odds with their Texas extended family. Every kid, I once told my oldest, has to do things their parents make them do. Growing up on a ranch in Alberta, I had to poison gophers. Growing up with your lesbian moms in Austin, you have to spend three days of summer vacation at an Unlearning Racism workshop. Deal? Deal. No, the queerest thing might be the three generations under our roof. That we live with Madge's beloved mother Barbara, eighty-nine as I write, omnicompetent military widow, devout Catholic, staunch Republican. For sure the queerest thing about our family is that I live with someone who watches Fox News. And she lives with me.

❧

We've lived together almost ten years. Barbara and I have each had occasion to say: "Thank you for putting up with me." We rub each other the wrong way almost every day. Almost every day, we respect each other and love the strong family we have made.

❧

How tired I am after a marital quarrel, especially when it happened overnight in a long, tedious dream. Under pressure of solstice darkness I have started taking Ambien again. Meditation and medication, and still I wake in tears.

❧

Queer family life is just life with extra paperwork. Renewing the youngest boy's passport yesterday at a federal office, despite the government shutdown. "We make money for the government, they never shut us down," said the clerk as we wrote her a check. We had checked all the boxes on the list of requirements, but with my name on the birth certificate and Madge's on the adoption papers, the clerk couldn't square the circle and we had to start over again. On his passport application, our child only has one mom. The government shut down the other one.

I feel crowded out of my house and also like everyone's leaving. Grieving my parents, all they'll never be to me. My dad's dementia has opened a new hole in his violence. He chased my sister down the street and hit my mom in the head, and I may never go back. Trying to abdicate the big-sister role without leaving my little sister holding the bag. Dad's been worse off for longer but suddenly Mom is using the word "overwhelmed." We share a birthday, but she forgot it.

The older boy said: "It's only the rest of my life." Three times he shrieked, his arms in the air: "I'm freaking out! I'm freaking out! I'm freaking out!" We are all seeking the man he is becoming in the actions of the boy, the baby who made us mothers, whose love must go to others now if we've done this right.

Despite our careful negotiations, the younger brother now calls the donor "Dad." Or sometimes Donor-Dad. Not sad, not bad, an honor, really, that our son doesn't dream that word might have any of the three of us freaking out, freaking out, freaking out.

So that I may repay my debt to the world, I acknowledge joy. Before dawn's light, I woke to make oatmeal for a child with studying to do. "Thank you," he said, "for being the best Mimi." Mimi is his name for me. To see myself as he sees me is a discipline, so later, I seat myself on a stony pillow. A flood of heat tunnels through my ribs, leaves my heart warmed, dissolved, re-formed as a net of golden fibers fragile and strong, along which the sound of the universe strums. O tell me, what was I looking for when I opened door after toilet stall door in the echoing empty locker room of which I so often dream. Each cubicle choked with filth. I thought, "I must get home." As ever, waste. As ever, cold clutch in the chest. As ever, the search. Said "Dramatic I" stagily, "this is just a dream." I woke again to a new locker room as clean as the Augean stables after the labor of Hercules. Pleased, I opened more doors. O tell me, what was I looking for. As ever, peace. As ever, safety. As ever, a guarantee. They say it is the most desired sight of all, the beauty of a loved woman who offers herself, the warmth of her tongue and lips, the welcome of the soft wet crevice between her legs, the restful mattress of her belly and thighs. Yet I say there is a waking more desirable. The fig tree planted instead of a vegetable garden. The warm gold tone of the spine's hum. As ever, joy. As ever, bliss. As ever, home. As ever, breath.

"Are you going to write a poem with fur coats in it, and hunting trophies," she asked after hearing what happened. I want to put my parents, dying, forgetful, careless and cold, violent and vulnerable, into this writing about being a parent. Yesterday I bought a damaged orchid, one of its blossoms torn but still with a whole delicate branch left to bloom. "It will last," I thought, and anyway orchids are meant to be torn by wind and falling sticks and nibbled by insects. The orchid is perfect because it finds the sun. This morning I raised the blind of my second-floor window and looked out to leafless twigs at the top of the elm tree in the yard. My fingers quivered to match their dance with the winter wind, to join with them from root to sapless bud. Everyone knows shadows cast in childhood are great energies that run amok through the generations. A stabbing blade of breath strikes deep into my mind. A nostril snarls to make room for more. A noise of engines fills the air, neither rising nor falling, neither advancing nor retreating, neither promise nor doom.

To relentlessly contest their privilege, yet stay heart-knit to the white boys I've been given to love. Yes, a phalanx of cranky and adoring women floats them. His favorite poet is Emily Dickinson. "Nice choice," I say, and he winks at me.

❧

Yes, they are lauded and launched by women, and they make us suffer. The younger is heart-stoppingly hard on himself, walking around and around the dining room table so he can memorize his monologue while also getting his exercise. The older dives deep into new love and again and again finds himself in over his head. If he breaks her heart it will break mine.

❧

The older boy loves pink so I make him a berry-frosted birthday cake. The sugar has formed hard lumps that I crumble in my fingers. I beat it with butter for longer than it takes to listen to an Indigo Girls song. I want to incorporate air, lighten the mixture, change the texture. My own mother taught me not to over-beat when I add the flour, keep the gluten strands intact. Gluten makes his brother sick, but it makes his own cake come out of the oven golden and risen. Labor of love, pick your poison.

❧

But I promised to tell you about Sunday dinner. It's a standing invitation for Dodo, the known donor. We gave each other a wide berth after the first boy was born, but once Dodo gave up his parental rights and Madge's adoption went through we all eased up. We had no idea it would look like this. We did it by feel. If you had told me at the beginning that my kids would be attending his fundamentalist nephew's family wedding, I would have been fretting all this time. "If I'm going to be a known donor," he said, "they need to know me." So he brings brownies every week and we make him dinner.

❧

A few years later our friend Tee said, "I'm staring hard at forty and I don't have a partner and I want a child. Can Dodo be my donor too?" We said out loud, "It's totally his sperm to give you!" And later murmured, just to one another, "but WE are those special sperm-donated, queer-created mothers." Still, we opened to the silver stream of living water pouring through and now there's someone new at Sunday dinner, two someones, Tee and her daughter. After the birth of our second child, Madge said to me—I was forty and exhausted—"we're not done! I know there's a girl waiting for us somewhere." Turns out it was Tee's daughter, the cherry on top of Dodo's Sunday brownies.

❧

Barbara sits at the head of the table, Madge at the foot. I chafe sometimes at my place on the side, but what is it I want that I don't have? We hold hands and sing about justice and kindness and God, no matter who else is there. And I send up a silent prayer: "thank you for putting up with me."

Baskets

MEGAN SNYDER-CAMP

My mother kept two of my father's baskets after the divorce and used them as trashcans. They were either from his days as a folklorist, made by someone who had a particular story to tell with the work, a particular reason for bending and weaving what was at hand, or they were storebought. More likely they were handmade: my mother would have known their value and wanted to take that from him in the divorce. More likely they were storebought: my father would have chosen to leave them behind.

Storebought, I hear an adoptive mom describe some of her kids, as opposed to her other three who are homegrown.

Things fit and then they don't, or they don't and then they do, or they do and they don't, both at the same time. I buy my clothes secondhand, my body warming the sweater's wool until it lights up with the smell of a stranger. Is it a weakness, how I lean into the absence of strangers, intimately, both of our arms in the sleeve at once.

When I was a girl I wanted to steal without stealing. In a craft store, I hid a basket in a basket in a basket, lidded it, and watched breathlessly as the checkout lady rang up just the one. What are you going to make today, she asked, as she was required to ask.

According to the books on simplicity, the ones who will be saved are the ones with the most to give up. One night my friends got drunk and talked about what they imagined polyamory to be: a fresher life, tulips on the table, the sort of love that would weave through what's already there, reinforcing rather than dismantling. A post-jealousy landscape with clear boundaries. Their conversation reminds me of foster parenting, how it looked to me before I entered it, the curiosity I felt, the clarity of my belief in a communal abacus. Slide a bead over, slide it back. Let me be a net, I thought, a thread, let me hold a gap for parents while they are getting things back together, let me step in to help families reunify.

Helping's not helping, my old landlord used to say, whenever I would try to fix something that wasn't mine to fix.

Why mother a child who already has a mother? The awkwardness of texting with that mother, the photobomb of my presence: why sign up for that? And then how ugly to speak of it, to offer up a platter to my friends, to lay out the fineness of what I am to be called or what we are together.

It's been thirteen years since my first child was born, three years since we began fostering. When my husband and I signed on—a yearlong process of trainings, interviews, visits—we thought of it like math: we already had three kids, the house was already a mess, so why not do this now, in the years when our lives were already childed-up? To attempt a sort of return to the wider extended family and community network that used to provide the mercy and slack parents sometimes need. To be part of a child's journey. To offer safety and time and possibly joy. I could become the mom of this house, the mom of certain weeks or years, hyphenated, alongside, one rope in a child's net, but not the center of the web. Last summer, in a Pollyanna-ish poly-mom moment, I hesitated in front of an "I love my moms" rainbow onesie at the GAP, thinking of the three women who have mothered my kid, all of whom are still in her life, and what it might look like to make that multiplicity visible, to wear it with pride. But if I were to celebrate that, what a jackass I would be, not only to the queer families for whom that onesie was intended, but also to my kid's mom, whose daughter was taken from her without her consent.

Two things neither my years of mothering nor all my foster parent trainings could prepare me for: how to try to mother a child in a pluralized way, and how to accompany a child in the wake of trauma. To be always consciously engaged in the act of repair, and yet to try not to stitch shut pain that needs to breathe. How when I talk about foster parenting it turns any conversation into snow, even here—I had hoped this would be the one in which you could see the joy, but it's mostly another one I can't put down—I mean the life I circle and circle, my mothering a vine, my mothering a thing that spreads if I'm not careful.

As a foster parent, I am the only one who chooses this life. The parents had their child, or children, taken from them, and will feel that loss forever, even if their child is eventually returned to them. When a child arrives in my home, they aren't happy to be here, or lucky. They have been separated from their family and brought into a system where enormous things will be decided, and re-decided, and broken, and perhaps rebuilt, by shifting groups of dedicated, overworked strangers.

Talking about this is tricky. A child's story is their own. And so what's left, what sits above the surface, at the place where my story intersects with the story of a vulnerable child, what's safe to tell, must seem odd and disjointed, a bunch of elbows.

Foster parenting challenges my use of language in ways I often don't see coming until I am midsentence, grabbing at air. Now that I'm a foster parent, I have three kids, or four, or five, or even six, depending. When they enter my poems, it's a challenge to balance a reader's desire for clarity alongside my need to leave some things unsaid. I am learning when to keep my mouth shut. How not to tell what isn't mine to say. Fostering is a path that binds the tongue, and in that silence, sometimes, oh the beauty. The flashes of childhoods I am lucky enough to get to dovetail my own days with, for however long. An unhurried look at a bumblebee by the curb. On the street no one can guess us, my youngest girls six weeks apart in age, carrying each other's songs on their tongues.

How can I write from inside this split-tongued life? I search for language that fits our changing family, words that cover us and allow us to claim a place within our community, without disclosing the confidential fact that some of our kids might be in foster care, and without erasing, or past-tensing, the primary connection my kids have to the families they were born into. I resist the invention of new language for this; what we are doing is not new.

But the words I once used to talk about my family, back in the day when my family was composed only of people who were simply mine, feel like shrunken laundry now, leaving us partially uncovered. Ours is a family that changes. Words that sometimes fit: *adjacency, expansion, alongsidedness, fluidity, unspoken loss, shimmering difference.* I am searching for the word that means mother not mother.

Writing Prompts

As you begin using the prompts in this book, we encourage you to use freewriting and become comfortable just getting all your ideas down in an initial messy draft, what Anne Lamott has famously called a "shitty first draft." A good way to get started can be to make a list of a bunch of ideas and then select the ones that have energy or heat around them—the ones that whisper to you that there might be more to say. After that first draft you can begin to refine and revise your work.

It might help you to have a dedicated notebook for your work. (Though many of our contributors describe writing on scrap paper, the back of a receipt or a grocery list, or recording thoughts in the notes section or voice recorder of their smartphone—so do what works for you.) Whatever path you take into writing, we think you'll be inspired by the poems and essays in this collection and bolstered by these writers' insistence that your voice and your perspective matter.

The prompts in this part will invite you to begin writing about your own life and experiences as a parent. Here, you'll find avenues into writing that begin with the tangible places and objects of family life, as well as prompts that invite you to use your creativity through metaphor and through speaking directly to the people you hope will understand your struggles and joys.

1) Many of these poems are rooted in a particular place related to parenting or family life and use specific, concrete language to describe that setting. In Catherine Pierce's "High Dangerous," this place is the

walk to the beach. Heid E. Erdrich's "Intimate Detail" is set among the plants growing by her front door when a delivery man arrives. Start by making a list of places that have been important to you in your parenting journey, and try to think of specifics: not just your kitchen, for example, but the high chair in the corner with applesauce crusted on it. As you write, focus on specific nouns, like the way Erdrich names particular plants ("cottage cosmos, nicotiana, / and bean vine"), or precise, surprising verbs, as in Pierce's descriptions of the bees that "ricochet in and out / of the clustered petals." You can also think about sensory details—descriptive language that draws on the five senses of touch, taste, sight, smell, and hearing.

2) Several other poems focus on specific objects associated with babyhood, childhood, and motherhood. Carrie Fountain's "To White Noise" functions as a praise poem for the white noise machines that guard her children's sleep. In "At the Museum of Trades and Traditions," Keetje Kuipers, whose child was conceived via IVF, considers both the objects displayed in the museum and "the tools that made me a mother." What objects have been central to your experience of motherhood? Write a poem that describes one or more objects and their significance for you and your family.

3) Several poems here make use of direct address. Victoria Chang's "Dear P." is a litany of wishes for and instructions to a child, things that a parent might think but not express aloud. In "Landscape with Clinic and Oracle," Lynn Melnick writes to her younger self. And in "Virgil, Hey," Camille Guthrie turns to the ancient Roman poet in a moment of exasperation with her adolescent children. Write a poem that directly addresses someone—whether it's your growing children, your past self, or a figure who might provide you with some guidance in a moment of difficulty.

   You might choose to establish rhythm, as Chang does, through anaphora, the repetition of words at the start of phrases. Chang uses "please" and "black" and "someday someone." Pick a few key words to repeat in the opening, middle, and end of your poem.

4) Remica Bingham-Risher's poem "We See *The Lion King* on Broadway, I Enter the Pride" captures a moment when a blended family comes together and the stepmother speaker of the poem notes that this moment is the culmination of years of time together. What moments have been significant in your own family's life? Like Bingham-Risher, de-

scribe one particular moment—perhaps a family trip or a milestone—in detail and end with an image that suggests what this moment has meant for your family.

5) Joy Ladin's "The Leopard" and Megan Snyder-Camp's "Permanency" both use metaphors to share something important about their families. Snyder-Camp describes how her son loves water bears, who "need nothing / have nothing and are everywhere," and this durability is in contrast with the shifting family configurations of foster parenting. In Ladin's poem, the leopard stalking its prey works as a metaphor for a dangerous variety of love, which "flings its kill over branches / in the jungle / that is your kitchen." What metaphors could capture something about your family life? Build a poem around these metaphors.

The Body and the Brain

MOTHERING IS BODILY WORK. PREGNANCY, BIRTH, and breast-feeding require enormous resources of energy and often transform one's relationship to both body and identity. Those who struggle with infertility devote months and even years of their lives to hormone treatments and invasive procedures. Those who enter motherhood through adoption, fostering, or a partner's pregnancy, and those who supplement or formula feed, are also enmeshed in the whole-body love and work of caregiving. Mothers with health challenges—their own or their children's—may experience the physical demands of parenting with even more intensity. This bodily labor can feel at odds with the work of writing, which is often seen as intellectual activity that requires quiet and isolation. The writing in this part examines the relationship between the body and the brain and points the way toward seeing writing and mothering as working in concert.

These poems portray an array of experiences of birth and early motherhood. Kwoya Fagin Maples, Laura Da', and Alexa Doran all write about caesarean birth. Maples notes her "collapsed belly" just after giving birth to her twins, and Da' places the work of the Shawnee mound builders alongside her newborn son's "ferocious cry." The hazy months of early motherhood are the subject of both Joan Naviyuk Kane's "When the World Was Milk" and Beth Ann Fennelly's "Latching On, Falling Off." These poems also consider difficulties on the path to motherhood, as in Monica Youn's "Blackacre," which portrays assisted reproduction, and Raina J. León's "We Never Talk about This: Chemical Pregnancy," about an early miscarriage. In Diannely Antigua's "Re-Education," the speaker chooses not to become a mother and takes Plan B. Together, these poems consider the mother's body as a site of trauma, heartbreak, tenderness, and joy.

Poems in this part also consider how mothering is shaped by chronic illness, mental illness, disability, and abuse. In Molly Spencer's "After Reading the Story of Assumption Chapel in Cold Spring, Minnesota," a mother grapples with the doctor's diagnosis of a disease that will be a "long growing / season beset by plague and fire, good years / and lean." In both Sherine Gilmour's "Pediatric Laboratory Feces Test #1" and Carolina Ebeid's "Veronicas of a Matador," the speaker is the mother of a child with autism; in Gilmour's poem, the diagnosis process is just beginning, and in Ebeid's, the son becomes enamored with the snippets of poems his parents read to him and wanders through the house reciting Marianne Moore. Two poems in this part specifically reference physical abuse and violence. Hope Wabuke's "In This Body, You're Disappearing" speaks of a mother beaten by her partner, and in Eugenia Leigh's "Gold," a new mother lives with the echoes of her father's abuse.

The essays here consider infertility, postpartum depression, and chronic illness. Throughout those struggles, they insist on writing as a vital tool for making meaning. Spencer's essay urges mothers to "do your own work first." Wherever you and your body and brain are on your motherhood journey, these pieces suggest that you are, as Kwoya Fagin Maples's poem concludes, "worth tenderness."

My Mother Bathes Me after I Give Birth

KWOYA FAGIN MAPLES

For Wanda Marie Ravenell

Washing my collapsed belly, crossing the soapy cloth over my
wilted shoulders and back is a familiar act for my mother, and
washing her child is like riding a bike, a thing she will not forget.

At first I feel something as deep as shame, standing naked and
framed by the backsplash of the shower, the remnants of the
anesthesia clattering through me.

I watch the blood pool between my feet before narrowing as it
moves toward the drain. My shoulders can no longer support the
weight of my mind. I can only look at the tiled shower floor and
not at any part of my mother's face.

My babies have been taken straight to the NICU from my body.
I kissed unfeeling kisses on their lips and faces, and before the
kisses dry, they are swaddled tight and wheeled away. I am
bleeding from their exit, my incision numb yet throbbing at the belly.

The nurse has said to allow the water to soak the bandage, and it
will fall off the incision. It does. While my mother soaps my arms
I wash between my legs with another cloth, astounded at the
blood. I glance at my mother what to do with the reddened cloth,
she says, *let it fall in the tub.*

Moments later a heap of soaking cloths near the drain. My
mother has asked for extra towels—warm towels, and she wraps
them around me when I've stepped out of the shower. She dries
me with the door shut to keep the heat in. When she moves the
lotion over my skin with her hands I breathe. I am an aching shell
but her touch says I am worth tenderness.

When the World Was Milk

JOAN NAVIYUK KANE

Seized between breaths the hard mother of the brain—
twice pierced through, atremble too with the anesthetist's
imprecision. I

could not walk for days
but fed, or tried to feed, shuffling flowers
stiff and white and dry as paper

for I could not lift a pitcher to refill
the water drawn out beneath them.
Men surround me, or will, all yellow

sclera, thunder & fallow.

from "The Black Maria"

ARACELIS GIRMAY

VIII.

How did it happen?
The boy. The cops. My body in this poem.

The body, bearing something ordinary as light   Opens

as in a room somewhere the friend opens in poppy, in flame, burns &
bears the child—out.

When I did it was the hours & hours of breaking. The bucking of
it all, the push & head

not moving, not an inch until,
when he flew from me, it was the night who came

flying through me with all its hair,
the immense terror of his face & noise.

I heard the stranger & my brain, without looking, vowed
a love him vow. His struggling, merely, to be

split me down, with the axe, to two. How true,
the thinness of our hovering between the realms of Here, Not Here.

The fight, first, to open, then to breathe,
& then to close. Each of us entering the world

& entering the world like this.
Soft. Unlikely. Then—

the idiosyncratic minds & verbs.
    Beloveds, making your ways

to & away from us, always, across the centuries,
inside the vastness of the galaxy, how improbable it is that this iteration

of you or you or me might come to be at all—Body of fear,
Body of laughing—& even last a second. This fact should make us fall all

to our knees with awe,
the beauty of it against these odds,

the stacks & stacks of near misses
& slimmest chances that birthed one ancestor into the next & next.

Profound, unspeakable cruelty who counters this, who does not see.

& so to tenderness I add my action.

Latching On, Falling Off

BETH ANN FENNELLY

I. When She Takes My Body into Her Body

She comes to me squirming in her father's arms,
gumming her fingers, her blanket, or rooting
on his neck, thrashing her mouth from side to side
to raise a nipple among his beard hairs. My shirt sprouts
two dark eyes; for three weeks she's been outside me,
and I cry milk to hear my baby—any baby—cry.

In the night, she smells me. From her bassinet
she wakes with a squall, her mouth impossibly huge,
her tongue aquiver with anger the baby book says
she doesn't have, aquiver like the clapper of a bell.
Her passion I wasn't prepared for, her need
naked as a sturgeon with a rippling, red gill.

Who named this *letdown*, this tingling upswing?
A valve twists, the thin opalescence spurts past the gate,
then comes the hindcream to make my baby creamyfat.
I fumble with one hand at my bra, offer the target
of my darkened nipple, with the other hand steady
her too-heavy head. She clamps on, the wailing ceases.

No one ever mentioned she's out for blood. I wince
as she tugs milk from ducts all the way to my armpits.
It hurts like when an angry sister plaits your hair.
It hurts like that, and like that you desire it.
Soon, soon—I am listening—she swallows,
and a layer of pain kicks free like a blanket.

Tethered, my womb spasms, then, lower, something shivers.
Pleasure piggybacks the pain, though it, too,
isn't mentioned, not to the child, drunk and splayed
like a hobo, not to the sleeping husband, innocent beside us.

Let me get it right so I remember: Once, I bared my chest
and found an animal. Once, I was delicious.

II. First Night Away from Claire

I forget to pack my breast pump,
a novelty not in any novelty shop
here at the beach, just snorkel tubes,
shark teeth, coconut-shell bikini tops.

Should we drive back? I'm near-drunk
from my first beer in months. We've got
a babysitter, a hotel room, and on the horizon
a meteor shower promised. We've planned
slow sex, sky watch, long sleep.
His hand feels good low on my back,
tracing my lizard tattoo. And he can help—
he's had quick sips before—so we stay,
rubbing tongues, butter-dripping shrimp.

Later, he tries tamely, but it's not sexy,
not at all—he'd need to suck a glassful
from each breast. The baby's so much better.
He rests. *It's hot*, he says, *and sweet.*
We're tired. We fall asleep.
I wake predawn from pain.

Those meteors we were too tired to watch—
it will be thirty years
before they pass this way again.

III. After Weaning, My Breasts Resume Their Lives as Glamour Girls

Initially hesitant, yes,
but once called into duty,
they never looked back.

Models-turned-spokeswomen,
they never dreamed they'd have so much to say.
They swelled with purpose,

mastered that underwater tongue,
translating the baby's long-vowel cries
and oozing their answer,

tidal, undeniable, fulfilled.
For a year, they let the child draw forth
that starry river, as my friend Ann has termed it—

then, it was time, stopped the flow.
They are dry now, smaller, tidy, my nipples again
the lighter, more fetching pink.

The bras ugly as Ace bandages,
thick-strapped, trap-doored,
too busy for beauty—

and the cotton pads lining them
until damp, then yeasting in the hamper—
all have been washed and stored away.

So I'm thinking of how,
when World War II had ended,
the factory-working wives

were fired, sent home
to cook for returning soldier husbands
when my husband enters the bedroom—

Aren't you glad? he asks, glad,
watching me unwrap bras
tissue-thin and decorative

from the tissue of my old life,
watching, worshipfully, the breasts resettle
as I fasten his red favorite—

Aren't you glad? He's walking
toward them, addressing them, it seems—
but, Darling, they can't answer,

poured back into their old mold,
muffled beneath these lovely laces,
relearning how it feels, seen and not heard.

IV. It Was a Strange Country

where I lived with my daughter while I fed her
from my body. It was a small country, an island for two,
and there were things we couldn't bring with us,
like her father. He watched from the far shore,
well meaning, useless. Sometimes I asked
for a glass of water, so he had something to give.

The weather there was overcast, volatile.
We were tied to the tides of whimper and milk,
the flotsam of spit-up, warm and clotted,
on my neck, my thigh. Strange: I rarely minded,
I liked the yogurt smell trapped beneath her chinfolds.
How soon her breath bloomed sweet again.

She napped, my ducts refilled
like veins of gold that throb though lodged in rock.
When she woke, we amped up our body language.
How many hours did she kiss one breast or the other?
I told her things. She tugged my bottom lip,
like sounds were coins beneath my fascinating tongue.

We didn't get many tourists, much news—
behind the closed curtains, rocking in the chair,
the world was a rumor all summer. All autumn.
All winter, in which she sickened, sucked for comfort,
a cord of snot between her nose, my breast.
Her small pillows of breath. We slept there, single-bodied.

Then came spring and her milk teeth and her bones
longer in my lap, her feet dangling, and, rapt,
she watched me eat, scholar of sandwiches and water.
Well, I knew the signs. I held her tight, I waded out,
I swam us away from that country, swam us back
to my husband pacing the shore, yelling and waving,

in his man fists, baby spoons that flashed, cupping suns.
It was a strange country that we returned to, separately—
strange, but not for long. Soon, the milk stops
simmering and the child forgets the mother's taste,
so the motherland recedes on the horizon,
a kindness—we return to it only at death.

Pre-Op

JORDAN RICE

While my mother argues against everything I am becoming,
        my son sleeps upstairs, his outline scrawled in grainy light

across the monitor. And my mother's gone, the dead line reeling
its single tone. My legs ache, and I fear another blood clot—

what could break from such small dams to aneurism.
        But the moon's brighter than I remember, like colder nights

when pacing the drive I stood all hours at the entrance, looking up
        the empty street, expectant as the antique dealer's wife

in Watervliet, months before they closed, confused behind her register
as I progressed through shelves of rusted tools—awl and auger, level

and saw, rows of hand-hewn wooden boxes, shot-holed signs
        for long-forgotten varieties of soda—

believing me her child, a family friend, finally a stranger, then apologizing
        for her queerness with the story of her stroke in a Chicago restaurant,

her headache drowning the server's voice, the room blacked to silence.
I settle in the rocker, searching each leg for knots beaded deep in muscle

and waiting for my son to wake with hunger, so I can gather and tell him,
        this is what people do for the inconsolable.

Earth Mover

LAURA DA'

Ferocious and sly, my mind's talon
plucks liquid movement from rivers,

arteries, ink, amniotic fluid, delicate webs of optical nerves.
Puckered prospect of the Caesarean veil.

My skin twisted in stainless steel pliers proves
the efficacy of the spinal block that dulls

my pain but leaves a cavity for the sonic panic
of my child heaved from my abdomen.

I close my eyes and roll hills,
churn rivers, press shovel to earth and brace

for the abrasion that draws the past
glistening into the present.

In the Ohio Valley, mound builders
left massive earthworks.

Enamored with the idea of excavation,
settlers pilfered through the soil,

sorted remnants: feather headdresses, flakes of mica, pot shards,
bone fragments. When asked to define

an effigy depicted in a perplexing mound—
the Shawnee described *a perilous being wrought*

like a massive panther swimming
through rivers with the power to destroy

and renew. Alligator Mound.
No. I net the past and future in panther skin.

My son's ferocious cry—fanged and clawed
grip on the skin of the toppling world.

I clamp down on the tributary's gush,
lay claim to our place here.

Laboring

CHANDA FELDMAN

from "But We Lived"

Equally a place of living and dying—*shadow land*,
the midwives called the labor. An ax slid
under the mattress to break the bridle of pain;
two straight pins made a cross fastened to
the pillow warding off haints; the placenta
swaddled and buried deep in a yard grave. Gifts
of eggs and crackers for the new mother.
No one asked to hold the baby in the first six weeks.

The whole time the baby was arriving the midwife
talked under her breath, calling on God
to guide her steps, comforting with Bible passages.
They'd give you teas: tansy when things were lagging,
pepper to clear the afterbirth, and for a stillborn,
mint to keep the woman's milk from coming in.

After Reading the Story of Assumption Chapel in Cold Spring, Minnesota

MOLLY SPENCER

The doctor says, Your disease is still ripening.
        Ripening? you ask, and feel your teeth slice late plums
    through to stone. You think of seeds swollen
into fat hearts of summered flesh, then storms
        of locusts shearing bare the fields.
    He says, It may be years. And you watch linens vanish
like dreams, swallowed off clotheslines.
        You see a boy. He is small. He gathers locusts
    like stones that might save him
on a roofless night in the woods. Ten cents a bushel,
        he'll have new boots for winter. The doctor says,
    This is the nature of your disease—long growing
season beset by plague and fire, good years
        and lean. You sigh
    against the hollow cheeks of the farm wives.
Their husbands are building a chapel
        to the Virgin, a hillside plea, small cape
    of prayer. You say, Please, I have built a roof
over my children's heads. It is close to collapse.
        You say it—ripening—, imagine a woman carved
    in stone above a doorway,
rising skyward, her hands
        held out to the locusts at her feet
    as if to say, Yes,
even this.

Blackacre

MONICA YOUN

one day they showed me a dark moon ringed
with a bright nimbus on a swirling gray screen
they called it my last chance for neverending life
but the next day it was gone it had already
launched itself into the gray sky like an escape
capsule accidentally empty sent spiraling into the
unpeopled galaxies of my trackless gray body

We Never Talk about This: Chemical Pregnancy

RAINA J. LEÓN

After *Solitary Boat* by Ficre Ghebreyesus,
with chorus from "Stay" by Carol Maillard
of Sweet Honey in the Rock

~ (coro)
the clock on the wall
says it's time to go

in the dream the knowledge pounced
and i felt that i was pregnant again
woke from sleep and felt the hard secret nut
the uterus in its first swell
just before sleep i had seen a shadow dog
in the corner between desk and television
i worried it had appeared to mouth your brother's essence and steal it away
i prayed over him
called on his angels and my grandmother as mine for protection
did it come for you instead?

~ (coro)
the clock on the wall
says it's time to go

days later when i learned you were no longer in me
flesh expelled in a blood tinged webbing of mucus
how the body shows a spoiled seed's end before the blossom or fruit
i saw a painting of a lone boat in a dark sea
there were no people
had they already drowned in their migration across troubled seas
with only the tubing garish yellow remaining
orbs abandoned to the latest hours
bridge lights lit far off

you who were a being of water and flesh and gold and wind
a breath slip, gone before a name could fix you,

i imagined you swayed in the boat
then a twisted seaweed pat in the tumble of invisible waves
then a pebble that falls too fast to be carried

~ (coro)
the clock on the wall

you were more than a number on a test i begged the doctor to give me
again regarded as insane for knowing my own body
and when she saw the proof said miracles do happen
as if the miracle was the numbers
my sanity a miracle
as if you were passively placed and not already animate with your lessons to teach
in form and unforming
as if

i ponder brush strokes
it may take me a lifetime to understand
someday i will seek you beyond my eye's sight
i will give you this poem
i will ask your name

i feel the light around me
you are in that light
on gilded water

~ (coro)

Re-Education

DIANNELY ANTIGUA

I listen to podcasts to learn about feminism,
watch porn to make sure I'm doing it right.
I dance on the bar because Coyote Ugly,
because these shoes, this drink.
I'm almost 30.
And I still think Bloody Mary is
a game with a mirror. Sometimes
she appears at 2AM. Sometimes she's
in the toilet, piss reflection before the flush.
There is a truth in this magic—
the time I took Plan B, then
the other time I took Plan B. I bled
for two months. There could've been
a mother in me. I told no one,
except the man at Tacos Lupita
who asked what I wanted in my burrito
and I think I said *baby*. I think I
spun around three times and whispered a name.
And there was no floor
when I fell, when a queen
flew from my womb. There was glass
and napkins, and the doctor
saying, *Wake up. Wake up.*

Again

JASMINNE MENDEZ

You want to know if I'd do it again. All over again. No. Not if I had the choice. Not the injections. Not the pills. Not the endless. Ultrasounds. Not the anxiety. Or the "will it take?" Or the "is there a heartbeat?" Or the "how many viable embryos?" No. Not again. Not for another. And not for a "because it's worth it." No. There are not enough of those for me. To do it. Again. I like. To be alone. To hold my body. To sleep in my body. To listen to what. My body needs. And it cannot. Won't. Doesn't want to. Do any of it. Again. The womb. Was fruitful. Birthing. Was tender. I loved what my bones. And my blood. And my skin became while pregnant. But I wouldn't do it. Again. I've lost. Too many. Things. To become a mother. Things. I would not have given up. Had I. Known. She is my breath. My body. Her body. I wouldn't give that up. Now. But no. I wouldn't. Won't. Can't. Don't want to. Do it. Again.

I Pump Milk like a Boss

KENDRA DECOLO

I pump milk on the side of the road where the grass is biblical green
as if first cousin to the cow, her pink and swollen tits immaculate

as the plumbing of a church organ sending up calls to god, brassy mesh
of notes, fermented and dank as kush. I pump milk with my bare hands

into a bar's bathroom sink, above which is a mirror where someone's
        scrawled
I Love Cricket Pussy and below that, Everyone Deserves to be Loved.

I look at myself under the fingered smudge, the bodily fluids spattered
like haikus and I pump as if my milk is propaganda,

fingers bowing across my chest like a pawnshop violin,
milky graffiti tagging the spit-clogged drain.

I pump like I'm writing my name in blood
which turns to the milk my child sucks dry, which she turns into blood.

I pump like I have a tattoo on my pudenda
that says Aerosmith backwards, I pump

as if my hands have teeth, one combat boot hitched up on the toilet seat,
each hiss of milk chanting like a choir *yes bitch yes*,

my tits bitten and salt-veined, as when my baby
took her first gulp of air, humming

from the engorged crevasse of me
like a herd of wildebeest, as if the hive of me could have burst,

the infrared honey, the *glop glop*
of afterbirth dripping down my left leg,

spittle and amen, amniotic residue
fluorescent with prayer—

Do men lactate is a popular Google search and I wonder
what would happen if they could, our presidents

lifting their offspring to their breasts in the deep pockets
of night, listening to the dribble of milk

sipped from the pulpit of their bodies. Tonight my breasts
became so engorged I said I'd pay someone to suck my tits

half-joking. But a woman who heard followed me to the bathroom, read me
a sex poem while I pumped my milk, leaning away from the need in her
    voice

and the milk came slow and I pumped and waited for her to finish
and a streetlight scribbled in the parking lot

and I know there is a price we pay for loneliness
and a price we pay to forget it and I dedicate my libido

to my younger self and this is how I want to live, milk-stained, a little bit
    emptied,
a little bit in love with the abundance of my body,

my milk pale yellow with a layer of cream
which I will save long after it's turned, praising its curdled glow

every time I open the fridge, as if its presence is enough to keep me safe,
as if it's enough to make me invincible.

C-Section

ALEXA DORAN

Sometimes when the room is made of oak

and I am made of flesh

the room and I mix like air and incense : our fusion a funnel of smoke

That's how you left my body, Buggy

Cloud ladled out of me.
All the other babies

puddling between their mothers' thighs

while you rose like any rainbow

a fountain of every light / but your own

Unfettered flume!

the sky spread into a cape around you

*It was better not to touch you
*It was better that the room was white and used
*That the surgeon whispered *trippy* as he felt the willow weight of you

Like all those plump bastards, young and hanging

from Michelangelo's roof

you were cherub chiseled in the ceiling

and I was artist-peasant-falling
beneath you

Son to say I was afraid

of the star cough covered in blood / of the birth of my son / of giving gravity its due

to say that I cannot huff and puff
enough to keep you afloat

is a version of the truth   that never reaches you   like blades
that rotate on a fan

all you hear is my breath below *choo choo*   *choo choo*

To My Brother, in Her Barrenness

MEG DAY

for Mitch

So this is poverty. So
immaculate conception
is all that's left. A family
walks five across down
Alice Street, little fingers
on a hand & the thumb
is kicking trash. What past
life gone wrong blessed
that womb's fruit, ripened
it into this uninhabitable
time? The second hand
has all but disappeared.
Who's to say we won't
ripen too: *stay* was a word
I finally knew after teaching
a mutt to do what I couldn't.
Will you put that fist in
the air with mine like a swear
you can't take back? C'mon
Brother: we must be near
the bottom of goodbye
by now. It's morning again
& outside a child is yelling
Not it! Not it! & someone
keeps asking, *Do we have to*
live through this again? It's you,
Brother. We don't.

In This Body, You're Disappearing

HOPE WABUKE

after Ocean Vuong

Then the Lord God used the rib from the man to make a
woman, and then he brought the woman to the man.
—Genesis 2:22

You need to believe it was for the love
and not its opposite. For to love
is to hold your heart outside

your body and inside
another, the red echo pulsing
through your marrow to sound what cannot
be heard.

❧

You, pulled
through the bones
by his desire,

You, your clay self molded
into the shape fitting
his desires.

❧

this is how we make   the mistakes our children inherit   how, that first night
the man returns clutching his weapons   baptized in the bones & the blood   of the animals
whose care you are tasked with   & the man holds you down & he—
& you stay   because you were made to honor & obey &   you both know
the man will do it again   & he does &
you stay.

❧

And the one in your belly you do not

yet know exists   is already
learning there are only two choices:
predator and   prey.

❧

See red. See nothing. Swollen,
his sweat dripped into your slitted
eyes, hold onto the sting of his salt against
your skin and know we will be legion
in the iterations of the becoming through
your belly—we are the belly of
the belly, repeated, infinite; formed in the vast
blackness of space, wombed
bones stuttered into being like stars.

❧

Night, always: his arrival; pulse, racing. *Run.*

❧

In the wanting to be safe was believing   the first man who said
his body would stand   between the world and yours   like your god promised
when gifting you   left anyway to stand alone   before serpentined satan
& evicted   body swelled   with child   you would have understood
his curse   was not in the pain of birth   but for us   your daughters in
line with another & the next   it would be   this singular weight
this rib of unboned promise   now separate   to bear the ripping
apart of the act of creation alone   because what is written inside the body
cannot be denied.

❧

And perhaps, the anger was not in the failed test of the apple, but that in giving you the act of creation you were made his equal, not the man.

❧

But how in the breaking

everything you gave

will be used

against you.

❧

But why would love set up love to fail?

❧

And if there is no memory of before violence
   was learned as love, there is
only the sounding of how, long before this
   baby is a wish inside your body
there will be no warning to
   know how others, much later
will seek out this cracking sounding of
   the fault lines in our bones with
the careful deliberation of a stormed wind moving
   across not just the waters,
sand or mud but the hardest, deepest rock
   to shatter further
and destroy.

Gold

EUGENIA LEIGH

I've become
the kind of creature who, on Sundays,
fills seven small boxes with a bevy of pills

to stick it out another week.
When will I be fixed enough
to hear my kid scream without tearing

my father's phantom hands off me?
How do demons, decades gone now,
still ravage me? Tell me

I am not the thing
my children will have to survive.
Tell me

the mob I inherited will not touch
my son. Yes, the cavalcade
of all that's tried to kill me

may forever raid my brain, but know
this: in my mother's first language,
the word for *fracture*, for *crack*,

is the same as the word for *gold*.
Every Thursday for twenty-one months
before my son was born,

a doctor trained me to put the gun down
and write.   I understand
I am one of the lucky ones.

Pediatric Laboratory Feces Test #1

SHERINE GILMOUR

I was given lab instructions and a tiny spoon.
I kneel on the floor, holding my son's diaper,
and measure the right amount

into each vial of unknown fluid, lethal fluid
labeled with his name by my own hand,
rank smell of formaldehyde in the air.

I was given lab instructions and a tiny spoon.
Plastic gloves. Fucked up world.
"Please act like tea leaves," I say out loud

my voice, alien in the room.
I want this shit to tell me how to help.
I kneel on the floor and measure the right amount.

Yeast shit, bacteria shit. Neurological impairment. Autism shit.
Possible heavy metal poisoning. Mitochondrial damage.
Could be he contracted something from me? From the hospital?

My sweet baby now asleep in his crib.
I think of how I fed him applesauce in a little bowl,
wiped his face, and kissed his cheek.

(Just these thoughts, and in my skin, I can feel
the warmth of him. His body
is my body. His body held to mine.)

I kneel and put the vials down, shaky, on the floor.
Lined up then sealed
in endless bags labeled "Toxic."

I was given lab instructions and a cardboard box.
I sit rigid on the couch, sun ticking like a clock
across my face, and wait for FedEx to pick them up.
Powerless shit. Powerful shit.

Veronicas of a Matador

CAROLINA EBEID

night said

After a diagnosis, one thing
becomes obvious: a good
patient is a patient patient.
I forget which is the superstition.
Trouble comes
in twos? Or in threes?
Night said: I am an ox
drawing my harrow.
Night said: I am a lacemaker
with a pincushion bouquet.
What were you expecting night to say?

yet why not say what happened

My son is autistic / My son has autism
I keep going back & forth.

Echolalia means the compulsive repetition
of meaningless phrases. Ditto goes for rock & roll.

Echolalia sounds more like a concert lute.
Lackofempathy could be a fern.

graceland

According to the Doctrine of Signatures,
some herbs will reveal their cures
by the image they take. An earache
will find reprieve on a shrub
of spotted lobes. Toothwort
resembles a sack of molars extracted & strewn
at the base of a tree. Take liverwort
for the liver. Take bloodroot. If you are afraid
to sing in front of people, locate the field
mellowing with Elvis shaped clover & graze.

imago

Adulthood has come to feel rather
like a mantle, a sudden soft
cambric weight, over the shoulders

weave in, weave in, my hardy
life. Mine is light & listless,
I sleep on the underside

of a leaf. And I am daily heaved
out of my chrysalis to brush
clean the fictive wings.

theory of the final girl

I wanted for my life
to stretch out everlastingly blue
& wide as the Urals
brains of beryl, kidneys of coal.

what are years?

My husband recited poems to calm
the boy to sleep. The boy would trundle
about the house with a line
from Marianne Moore
in his mouth on repeat: *satisfaction*,
he'd blurt out, *is a lowly thing, satisfaction*
is a lowly thing, & my husband would reply, yes
how pure a thing is joy, & it was satisfaction
the boy felt talking those words aloud
he'd memorized, that's how persons
behave, they go in & out of rooms
speaking words to one another,
in & out of doors, with words like hello
hello alfresco, hello you grassy inquiries
I have the greenest replies.

homo ludens

The boy rhymes shadow to meadow.

What does *fear* rhyme with? *Here.*

What does *there* rhyme with? *Mare.*

How about *sweater? Water.*

What does *alone* rhyme with? *A phone.*

What does *glory* rhyme with? *Story.*

weilian

With all the books
I've read, my
shadow makes
a heavy thing,
like a desert
mammal having just
eaten a creature
smaller than itself,
that had been eating
a creature even smaller.

i.e.p.

When did it dawn on you that your child was autistic?

It wasn't dawning; it was dusking on us, always dusking.

What was it like discovering your child has autism?

Other parents use figurative phrases that express a single, painful blow to the body: "like being bashed in the face with a bat," "like being hit by a train." For me, there was no bat or train. There was something like a photo-negative. The future presented itself like celluloid strips of negatives in a shoebox. Brightness & shadows became inverted, walking through my future city. The street lamps would radiate dark cones of light, & the sidewalk trees in front of row houses, frosted in the negative-white.

How would you describe a typical day with an autistic child?

I no longer search for a future in shoeboxes.

❧

through a glass, darkly

My friend, the baker,
insists we are dark to ourselves.
There in the aisles of lighting
fixtures suspended from the ceiling,
even among the carmine-dawn
azaleas, we are in the dark, looking
at our many breeds of darknesses.

❧

of the nimble turn of the head

It gives me an unmistakable joy
to see my baker friend snap apart
a knob of dough then flour it again.
I think of faraway hail spraying
on lakewater. There should be
a word for the kind of handsome
incorporation this is.

❧

measuring water's depth by sound

When I fell in love, I spoke
as a child & dressed as a child.

I developed a peculiar
inclination to pilfer guest soaps

molded into pinecones or robins' eggs
or little race cars. I lifted a lavender

heart, not the form inside
your ribcage—if I could just peer in

as through a glass, I'd say yours
looks like something from the sea.

letter to the Corinthians

But my most
magnificent
self, she runs
through a grass,
larkly.

Ode to Disappointment

ZEINA HASHEM BECK

Today, you are determined
to know about the soul. You decide you'll go
to an afternoon workshop in a bookstore with windows.
At the coffee shop, your daughters play XO
& you explain a diagonal trajectory is also possible.
So many beautiful things go downward,
like your daughters' hair, lightbulbs, breasts,
& some plants here, hung from the ceiling.
You realize you don't know the names of plants.
The small one on your table is a cactus,
but what's the one in the corner called, or the leaf
powdered in cacao on your coffee? Is this a sign
of growing old? To contemplate plants & acquire
a love for watermelon juice? To consider piercing your nose
or be seized by the brightness of this spoon, the ceiling lights
inside it like fishing boats? The waitress
is also a photographer & keeps a camera on the side.
She asks the couple in front of you (the guy strokes
his girlfriend's triceps) if she can take their photo.
Your daughter has red velvet cake in her hair,
your husband says he needs to pee. You go home,

answer emails & try to straighten your spine.
Your daughter figures out how to read "exactement,"
but can't tell the difference between 67, "soixante-sept,"
& 77, "soixante-dix-sept." You blame the French. You shout
dictation words across the living room & tell your kids no,
you're not making fries, they should eat salad.
You wonder whether it's wise to start asking them
to like salad when you have an appointment with your soul
in an hour. They agree to cucumber & grilled halloumi.
Before you leave, you ask your husband
if you look OK & he says your hair's too oily.
You run to the shower & tell yourself it's appropriate

to arrive a little late, with clean wet hair & no makeup
to a workshop on the soul. You throw in a wooden bead necklace.
As you walk out, your husband wonders why you insist
on going that late anyway. Don't listen. Get in the car & speed up.
You park & run to the bookstore in the heat.
There you are, with your wet hair your sweat your
wooden necklace your chipped nail polish, you are here
& the door is locked. The session's been cancelled.
All day the day's been telling you this
isn't working, stay home. You never really know

whether God wants you to give up or go on.
On the way back, you call your friend & she doesn't
pick up. You order a latte & the coffee tastes burnt.
You play backgammon with your daughters,
remind them to brush their teeth.
You rarely watch TV, but tonight you flip:
a movie about demigods, a swimsuit contest.
You order French fries & go to bed late.
Your husband walks in, bends down to kiss you
& noticing a loose thread coming out of your shoelace
on the floor, picks it up. He flicks on a lighter
& it's not the whole shoe that burns, just the thread.

Terrell Owens Private Messaged Me

KHADIJAH QUEEN

TERRELL OWENS PRIVATE MESSAGED ME ON MYSPACE I didn't believe it was actually him but he insisted & said I had a nice smile I returned the compliment that was way back when his career was promising & his body fat must have been at zero & when I said how cool it was that our sons have the same name I didn't get anymore all caps messages

Final Neon

SHAMALA GALLAGHER

Last night I ate neon seeds of sugar, late.
The bag from a worn station.
The gas pumps lurking
outside, large witness. Inside
waiting to see if the numbers
would blaze into a win.
I bought my Chewy Sweet Tarts
there, the bag purple
-battered, blue. $1.79. Outside
beneath the dark the blossoms
stayed wide-mouthed, like women
talking late. But I was alone.
City at the world's end:
time gone to soft dark.
The belly-child kicking.
Wanting out. Wanting out
for an instant with the blossoms.
Before the dark closes.
I drove home, twitching sweet-sick.
I won't eat that sugar
again. When the end is soon
you can surrender your vices.
I don't want a drink.

Confessional

RACHEL ZUCKER

This afternoon I've got a meeting with ________ ________ to tell her that the poem in which I call her my ________ ________ has been destroyed & I'll never publish it or read it at a reading because I'm done writing about anyone I work with, she has my word.

In a lecture I wrote, I say I've been influenced by photography more than poetry & spent years writing poems in response to photography's characteristic concerns. I say my career in poetry is one long synesthetic mistake. Now you can skip the lecture that anyway you weren't planning on attending. Also, the lecture's not really about photography & this isn't a poem.

My new friend Monica just texted me. I'm allowed to use her name because she's not a poet & I don't work with her & I haven't yet made that promise to ________ ________. Monica's very beautiful & intimidating & I like her because, even though we haven't ________ ________ together, we admitted to each other in low voices, in the dry goods aisle of Whole Foods, that we each like to ________ ________. I don't remember how the topic came up & can't say what Monica & I like because we're moms & it's not legal so I shoot blanks to protect her.

In my second lecture, the one about the legacy of confessional poetry, I get into it with Anne Sexton who is a terrible mother but a better poet than most people think. I talk about Lowell, Plath, Snodgrass but not so much Berryman. In the end, the lecture's mostly me looking at Sexton looking at Sexton & at her daughter & her mother who are also Sexton.

Sexton, as I said, is a very good poet & a very bad mother. I say "is" because mothers can be bad even if they're dead. My mother is. Bad & dead.

"As if it were normal / to be a mother and be gone" wrote Sexton.

Meanwhile ________'s mother has ________ which is sad & she would not like anyone to know.

I've got a poetry reading tomorrow with ________ & ________ who are excellent poets & intimidate me. Also, I love them & they are generous & by generous I mean not easily offended, which is a kind of love, don't you agree?

I don't know what to read. I'm sick of that new poem about my son worrying about death & the photographer Sally Mann & ________ has heard that already. I could read the poem about ________'s death, the one in which I use people's initials instead of names so as not to offend them but ________'s brother suggested I change the initials to different initials & I haven't done that yet.

An editor, by which I mean ________ ________, suggested I take the names out of my book. Can't you do the same thing without using names? he asked. So I took out the name of a famous poet I didn't know but kept dreaming about. The poems were kinder then or maybe crueler. They were definitely not the same. They were more about me & not about what had happened to the poet's daughter.

I wonder, I said to the editor, If naming is a kind of love? But the editor said, Hasn't he suffered enough? Tell them about the time you took out the names and it made the poem better, says the editor.

Lowell's poems were a "ghoulish operation on his soul" said M. L. Rosenthal & Adrienne Rich called Lowell's disclosures "bullshit eloquence," I said in a lecture.

If you don't have anything nice to say don't say anything, says everyone.

I say nothing for five minutes. Then I say, By the way I was paid $________ to write the lectures but it's *gauche*—pardon my French—to discuss money.

Just then ________ calls. I say, You really don't want to talk to me right now. She could hear tears in my voice & said, What's up? I told her I'd been rejected from ________ & ________ & would not be spending any weeks writing in the woods waiting for a covered basket of lunch. Also I did not get a ________ & I had not been invited back to teach at ________.

All that's not real! she shouted, which is something ________ never does, You get everything! Even the *New Yorker*! I wanted to hang up I felt so ________ but I knew she was right, this was not real. I felt ________ & ________, which felt all too real. Later ________ would apologize & say she was not herself but she *was* herself & I knew I should feel ________ of myself.

I mean really, what is it I don't have that I want? I ask myself.
That's the wrong question says ________.

If this is not a poem can I read it tomorrow at the reading?
If this is not a poem what is it?
A way to spend time with me?
A way for me to waste your time?
We voyeur each other & I perversify my proclivity to unprevaricate.

________ will not like the way I disparage myself in this way. ________ ________ will not like the way I am clearly talking about ________ & ________ & ________ & what will the gay guys think?

Does it offend everyone equally? asks ________.
Does that make it all right, I ask?
Without seeing the poem I have no way to know, says ________ but ________ doesn't have time to read the poem or hear it on the phone.

Without the poem I have nothing to show of myself, I say.
Do you mean "for yourself"? ________ asks.

I have nothing other than these lectures. (I almost wrote "which cost me my right arm," but didn't write that because that's not true although writing them has felt like ________ & has been hard as shit & fucked up my language, which is why I just wrote "hard as shit," which is a stupid thing to write. At the very least I should write "hard as old shit" since fresh shit isn't hard at all. "Hard as old shit" is more precise but is not something a real poet writes in a real poem.)

I write: "My son is very boring. To be more precise, I find being with him boring."

He wants to talk about soccer or Star Wars or Ellen DeGeneres, none of which interests me. I did, however, like the new Avengers movie because Mark Ruffalo & Robert Downey Jr. are hot as hell or hot as shit or hot as ________. I'm allowed to name them in poems because they're celebrities & also this is not a poem.

just write "often"
just write "like"
just write "the way the light [dot] [dot] [dot]"
say "landscape" or say nothing

For the record I, too, am a bad mother. Actually, I am an amazing mother, but all I want to do is work.

The other two sons are not boring. To be more precise, I find being with them enormously stressful.

I sometimes often find the way the light the landscape. Haha.

All I want to do is work.

"Perverse" as in: a deliberate, obstinate desire to behave in a way that is unacceptable.
As in: T minus minutes to soccer.
Or: roll two sheets of paper together—black & any other color—tape the seam = makeshift light saber.

The most interesting thing about me is ________.

That last blank has been left blank not because I am afraid of hurting someone's feelings or that it will negatively affect my career but because there is nothing interesting about me. If I were not practicing discretion I'd say the only interesting thing about me is my compulsive confessing.

Dear Anne Sexton
you were a bad mother
I am a better mother
than you were
bully for me

that's not saying much
on the other hand
you are a better poet
so many are this is not
false modesty
this is the truth
which no one
asked me for

After hearing my lecture on photography, Colin said I could not use the word "truth" without indexifying the term. I have no idea what Colin means & here I use his real name as a way of calling him out & to protect myself from the shame of believing in truth. If I can't say "truth," fuck it, I'll write "Colin" even if he is the boyfriend of my dear friend & might not like being in this poem. There I go again calling everything a poem!

I'm sick of my "I" & "she" pronouns, sick of what an editor called "the role of authenticity in your work" in which "role" means pretending something is something else, in which "you" means I. For example I am not actually sick when I say being a woman is ________ to me all these babies later. When I say being straight & white *wah wah* [dot] [dot] [dot]

It is despicable to be so ________. I mean really it is ________ to be so ________.

After my lecture on the legacy of confessional poetry my fifteen-year-old son said, So your lecture's about how we should feel sad for unhappy white women which you are? Everyone laughed. My son is very funny & smart. Not often hardly boring.

It turns out my sons are my best work but all I want to do is work.

Put it in the book! says ________, about a book we are & are not writing together, a sequel to our book about birth. This one will be about sex & middle age & we will say all the things we did not say before which will be very difficult to do after I make my vow. Oh me & my upcoming meeting! Will ________ ________ believe I've seen the error of my ways? Not if she comes to this reading.

What I want is a socially acceptable financially viable reason to be away from my children for weeks & weeks & weeks & weeks.

Last night I dreamed I was trying to get the Husband to have sex with me & every time he acquiesced it turned out we were in public. Despite the fact that no one seemed interested in watching us, he kept stopping because he was not into having sex in public & we ended up (in the dream) watching a movie with ________ & ________ & ________ put his hand on my leg & it occurred to me that this might be what I'd long ago experienced as a come-on although even in the dream the phrase "come-on" was so remote I kept thinking it wasn't the right idiom. Meanwhile, ________ had his hand on my leg & I thought (in the dream) at this point there is *no way* I would say no to *anyone*, which is not the same exactly as wanting to say yes to ________, but looks a lot like it because of course ________ *is* "anyone."

________, who shouted at me because I get everything even the *New Yorker* & with whom I am & am not writing a book, has ________ sex. She has it a lot & writes about it. I know this because she tells me all about it. Actually she tells me as much as she thinks I can handle, which is not very much. Also, I just read her new book which was supposed to be about her dead baby but has an awful lot of sex in it none of which is awful. In fact, I just read her poem about a student she had a crush on & how she wondered if her instructions in workshop were a kind of come-on which reminded me of my dream & also of my vow never to write a poem like that again at least not after my meeting which is in only a few hours. From now on I will only write about Mark Ruffalo & Robert Downey Jr. & I will not listen to my friend when she says if I want my needs met maybe I need a new partner so there we are:

Me & my ________ friend & her ________ poems & mine, although this is not a poem.

> Dear Mom
> I wrote two lectures
> one about photography
> & one about confessional
> poetry but they were not
> about those things
> both lectures were
> veiled ways of

explaining to you
why I insisted on
publishing a book
you didn't want me
to publish
it is difficult to
explain this to you
because you are
dead because you died &
the last thing you said
to your therapist was
"Tell Rachel not to
publish the book"
& I did anyway
I thought Dad had
lost his mind
when he said
"I *am* upset
Diane died—this
makes it much more
difficult to speak
with her."
I called my
stepmother to say
please deal with
Dad I couldn't
deal with anything
not myself not my
sons I had become
a woman who had
killed her own
mother but Dad
was right it *is*
more difficult
to speak to you
but I keep trying

Dear Mom
I think I have to
write the story of
what happened
this time without
research without
indexifying anything
if I even knew what
that meant I think
I will never be able
to write a poem
until I can
explain myself
to you which I
never can

Perhaps that's why I'm stupid enough to swear I'll never write another poem about anyone I know or use names, only my own maybe not even my own even if it means I show up to the reading with nothing new nothing mine nothing "true."

I almost wrote love cancer Wayne Jason Arielle 40K Yaddo MacDowell Guggenheim Daniel enraged ashamed exposed torture elitist crazy obnoxious privilege narcissistic libidinous lusty but stopped myself just in time.

More, More

JASMINNE MENDEZ

I pull the empty red spoon out of Luz María's mouth. It fumbles out of my right hand—again. I cannot clutch my fingers around it—it is small. I feel small. Luz María opens her small mouth. Her sticky wet pink tongue reaches out like dragon fruit tentacles exploding in my direction. Her chin juts forward. She is a baby bird waiting for worms. Her palms open and close—open and close. This is her sign for *more.*

¿Más? ¿Más? I ask. Her head bobbles left and right then up and down as she tries to nod yes or no.

I set the spoon inside the bowl and fold my hands into shadow puppets. A left and right mouth that opens and closes. I am trying to teach her baby sign language, because that is what all good mothers do these days—isn't it? My left hand becomes a less than symbol. My right hand becomes greater than. I tap my fingertips together.

Más. Más, I say.

I use three fingers instead of five to sign—*more, more*—because my scleroderma has left me without. Without a right hand middle fingertip—without straight knuckles—and with only limited mobility of my joints. My middle finger is rounded and smooth like a doorknob. My ring finger tilts like the leaning tower of Pisa.

After trying to sign "more," I scoop up the red spoon with all the fingers of my right hand, because my pincer grip is not as precise as hers anymore. I trace a letter *C* in her food bowl and fill the spoon up with just enough to feed her. My skin pulls and tightens, an overstuffed trash bag bursting at the seams. A pulsing throb beneath my nails. Then—a small tremor. A tiny earthquake inside my wrist and a knuckle buckles under the weight of the spoon. The food tumbles and falls out of the spoon and onto the crumb filled tray table—again.

Her soft baked potato fingers reach for the clump of green mush I have spilled on the tray. Her palms smash it down and she giggles. She is learning to understand the world by how it feels in her hands. Sometimes the world slips through her fingers. Sometimes she can hold it firm—throw it—bang it together or put it in her mouth. Sometimes she wants to carry more than her hands can hold. Her hands have not betrayed her yet—and I hope they never do.

I wipe the food away. I am used to making messes. She reaches for the plastic red spoon. I let her hold it for a moment. I let her feel what it feels like in her unsteady hands. She lifts it up to her nose—nope, that's not right—she lifts it up to her eyes—still too high—she lowers it down to her chin.

Almost. You almost got it, mi'ja.

She's made a mess all over her face. I do not wipe it away. We both laugh. With my good hand, I pull the spoon out of her tight fist and say:

I have to learn how to feed you now, mi'ja. *Mami's hands are not as strong as yours—but I promise I will try.*

My right hand doesn't bend and twist like it used to. My right hand doesn't hold or fold or fist or shake or clap or lie flat like it used to. My right hand is jealous of the left—so pretty, so perfect, so straight, so able to hold and fold and twist and bend and turn and pinch. My right hand misses scratching and saying hello.

So what is "more" when your fingertips have gone missing? When they curl into themselves and do not touch?

What is more when you always feel less than? Less than good enough because you drop things. Less than good enough because you cannot tie your shoes or open a can of soda. Less than a perfect mother because the buttons on her shirts are too small to thread between your fingers. Less than because the doctor wants you to tilt and wrap your too short stubby amputated digits around a bottle that is just too big for your hands and her tiny baby bird mouth.

Before my daughter was born I used to berate and belittle my hands for all they could not do. Stupid hands. Crippled hands. Tired hands. *Malditas manos. Pinches manos. Odio a mis manos.* I hate my hands. Fuck my hands.

But after twenty-seven hours of labor, when the doctor cleaned her off and placed her on my bare breathless chest and said, "she's perfect, she has ten little fingers and ten little toes, she's perfect," I knew then that I wanted more for her than what I had ever allowed myself to have. More confidence. More joy. More kindness. I needed her to know that even if she didn't have ten fingers or ten toes, she would be perfect.

So, I stopped berating my hands and I started wrapping them in grace and patience. I gave myself hand massages with lavender oils and eucalyptus. I bought expensive gold and silver rings with quartz, moon crystals, jade, emerald and larimar stones to channel the goddess in me. I thanked my hands every morning for holding just enough water to wash my face with. I thanked my hands every night for tingling, aching, bending, breaking, and being just enough.

My daughter will learn that she is more than enough.

Monstrous Mothers: Maternal Guilt, Rage, and Writing

CHELSEA RATHBURN

When my daughter was born, after a highly stressful, complicated pregnancy that required surgical intervention, we had no social or professional support: my husband had to return to work the day after we got home from the hospital, my parents left a day or two later, and our local friends meant well but didn't know the sort of help we needed, at the time having no children of their own. We seemed to become invisible overnight.

I developed severe postpartum depression, though I couldn't say so at the time. My story didn't match what my female relatives had told me, their fantasies of drowning their babies or having them disappear. But my story also didn't match the adorable pictures of placid newborns others were posting on Facebook. Most days, left alone with a fussy infant who screamed every second she was not being held or nursed, I was lucky if I managed to brush my teeth. I lived in a terrycloth bathrobe that reeked of sweat and sour milk.

At night, nursing in the dark, I would think over and over about killing myself. I did not tell my husband, because in my state I imagined he would take my baby away or put me on medication that would render me unable to nurse. Nursing was the one thing I could do easily, even if the act seemed to make me insane. So I nursed in the dark and thought about shooting myself. This was all done in a very abstract way. I did not want those I loved to deal with my body. I did not want my daughter to grow up motherless, even as I suspected she'd been born into a family with the worst sort of mother. No, I simply wanted to cease to exist.

Around this time, someone sent me a book of poetry about birth subtitled "An Eloquent and Ebullient Celebration of the Miracle of Life." I wanted to throw it across the room. These feelings intensified for months and months, and over time my invisibility and grief were mixed with guilt and rage. I still get flashes of it when I'm in confined spaces with my child. Over this most recent winter break, I was confined in a never-ending game involving cupcakes and Disney princesses. There it was. I felt like a trapped animal, sad and angry, ready to chew my own leg off while my daughter insisted "Again!" with her big eyes and bright smile.

This is a long way of explaining how I found myself a little in love with Eugene Delacroix's *Medea*, a painting I came across when my daughter was two, while preparing lecture notes on Euripides's tragedy. Looking at Medea's face—first on my laptop screen and later in person, after I'd begun writing poems about her, in Lille, France, on a trip that marked the end of my long illness—I felt as if I, at last, were *seen*. Someone saw me. Someone understood. Never mind that the someone understanding was a construction, or that she'd been captured on canvas just before murdering her children, or that she was painted by a man, or that the man who had painted her was notorious for his difficulty with women and perhaps his distrust of his own mother.

I began writing about Medea as a way of accessing my experiences with postpartum depression and maternal ambivalence, and I continued writing about the maternal body as a way of saying to other women, *you are not invisible. I see you.*

The Quiet Part: On Poetry, Race, Mothering, and Silence

ERIKA MEITNER

Our youngest son is black and we are white and there is always a (white) mother on the beach or at the playground or in the mall who will ask me when we are going to tell him that he's adopted—as if he didn't have the same powers of observation as an adult—as if the differences in our appearance might have somehow escaped his notice.

The first time someone ever said anything negative to us about our (black) son, it was a (white) man—a kid, really—maybe nineteen or twenty, who walked past us sitting at a bus stop in Belfast, Northern Ireland, and said (under his breath, but clearly) *fuck your family* and kept walking as if he hadn't said anything at all, and we looked at each other (my white husband and I), to see if we had both heard that, to make sure it was real. We were (as the saying goes) struck dumb.

It was nearly the same silence I felt weeks earlier when my older (white) son came home from school and said that when his (Protestant) teacher asked the class to raise their hands if anyone had family directly impacted by World War II, he didn't raise his hand, though my (Jewish) mother was born in a refugee camp in Stuttgart after my grandparents survived Auschwitz and Mauthausen, Neustadt-Glewe, and Ravensbrück, and how could he not know about this displacement, this torture, our involvement as victims and survivors except that I never told him—I assumed it would be part of his DNA, and he would just know via osmosis, this suffering and trauma and silence and silence and silence.

"Attention, taken to its highest degree, is the same thing as prayer. It presupposes faith and love," wrote Simone Weil, and the poetry I write is the poetry of attention. I record the things of this world (often as they happen) to make sense of them, weave disparate things together to create connections, and sometimes in my poems I tell secrets or write about things that are often left unsaid in real life. These days, people call this *saying the quiet part out loud*. People call this "confessional poetry" or tag the work as *brave* or *honest*. Wikipedia reminds me that the term confessional was first used by M. L. Rosenthal in a 1959 review of Robert Lowell's *Life Studies*; confessional poetry went "beyond customary bounds of reticence or personal embarrassment."

There are parts of my (black) son's story that I am not allowed to share (said our social worker), which have nothing to do with reticence or embarrassment or race, and everything to do with the fact that he's adopted, and every adoption has loss behind it, and the social workers reminded us constantly that his (back)story belongs to him and him alone, which seems simple to remember, but also easy to forget.

There's that story my rabbi used to relay often at high holiday services about the man who was told by his rebbe to take a feather pillow and cut it open—scatter the feathers in the wind—then gather them back up, to show him he could never make amends for the damage his words had done, but that was about malicious lies and not the truth. What happens if the truth is harmful—unable to be unknown again?

In twenty hours of adoption agency training we were told to be prepared for questions in the supermarket checkout line from strangers about our (black) son because we would be a *conspicuous* (multiracial) *family*, and they gave us sincere or snappy answers to questions like *where's his real mother?* and *how could she have given up such a beautiful child?* and *isn't he lucky?* and *does he speak English?* and *do you have any children of your own?* but no one at the agency told us what to do about the (white) guy walking past us at the bus stop in a foreign country where bigotry normally stems from politics, from ethno-religious nationalism, but not race, as Northern Ireland is approximately 98.6 percent white, though its history means that my students in Belfast had a broader knowledge of the U.S. civil rights movement than my students in the United States, where there are protests in the streets—where people have been marching for months upon months upon years to protest the killings of unarmed black boys and men and women by the police in Ferguson, Cleveland, Staten Island, Baltimore, Minneapolis, Louisville, Kenosha, and where else?

There will (unfortunately) be more elsewheres and I have tried to write poems about my fear for my (black) son, about how to keep him alive past his teens, about the protests I am able to attend and those I am not, but even the act of writing a poem as his (white) mother feels like I'm somehow exploiting him for my (white) art, as an easy way in to a complicated issue where I'm meant to listen and amplify the voices of my (black) friends and colleagues, since I have white privilege—I am white privilege—though that privilege won't protect my (black) son when he's old enough to be out in the world on his own. In Northern Ireland, no one ever asked us questions about our (black) son, like *Where is he from?* and *How much did he cost?*

Maybe this had to do with the culture of silence around personal information of all kinds, especially in Belfast. My students explained that people go to great lengths to avoid asking each other things we consider basic in America, like *Where are you from?* or *What school did you attend?* not because the answers easily identify their backgrounds and maybe allegiances and could possibly create uncomfortable tension between drinkers or partygoers, classmates or acquaintances, but because the questions themselves are actually a violence, a litmus test—because in the past, people have been killed when they answered one way or another. In Jewish law, all things are considered secret unless a person says otherwise. This is why (in Exodus) God constantly says to Moses, *Speak to the Children of Israel and tell them*, since if God had not specifically said this to Moses, Moses would be forbidden to repeat his words.

Moses—himself adopted by Pharaoh's daughter, who plucked him from the river Nile—freed the slaves and led them to the promised land but couldn't cross over with them. When I was a child, we read about this exodus with my family during the Passover Seder, where there were topics my grandparents kept secret and never spoke about (like their slave labor for the Germans or the family members who went to the gas chambers or the story about my grandmother euthanizing her own infant daughter) because of the shame implicit in being a victim, and the sheer horror of their testimony, and the part I'm leaving out is the way (maybe at the Seder table or maybe not) they used Yiddish to talk about money (*gelt*) and black people (*schvartzes*) and anything else that fell into the taboo category of things that were not too secret to be talked about at all.

The Talmud tells of a student who revealed a secret he had heard twenty-two years earlier, with the consequence that he was immediately banished from his house of study (Talmud Sanhedrin 31a). There is no time limit on secrets. In Exodus, Pharaoh's daughter said *I pulled him out of the water.* She said, *This is one of the Hebrew children.* She said, *Take this child, nurse him for me, and I will pay you.* When we first adopted my (black) son his skin was so light that people on Facebook said things like, *I didn't know you were pregnant*, under the photo I had posted of him sleeping in his car seat. My (black) neighbor told us his skin would turn darker, match the color on the inside of his tiny ears, and it did, and almost no one now will explicitly point out that our (black) son is a different race from us except for kids in preschool who sometimes asked me why my (black) son is brown or has brown skin or is a different (darker) color than the rest of our (white) family, and if I say *he was adopted and had a different first mom* they would ask (even when he was a baby) if he had to work in an orphanage (thanks, Disney!).

Right after we adopted my (black) son, my (white) son asked if his brother was Native American and I answered the way the agency taught me—I asked, *why do you think that?* and I don't remember what he answered, but my question didn't open the door to a frank conversation about race the way the agency told us it might, since he was five, but I do remember (clearly) the time I was listening to the radio and my (white) son was in the back seat and we pulled into the Food Lion and I left the engine on for a few minutes to hear NPR report on the grand jury in the Ferguson case and my (white) son wanted to know more about the radio story so I told him about Michael Brown, about the police shooting and his (black) body lying in the street for hours and hours and why people were angry, and my (white) son said *we can never let ________ go to Missouri*, and I had to tell him that this happened / was happening / will happen in other places too, and he said *we'll stay here* (in Blacksburg, in rural southwest Virginia, in Appalachia) because *it's safe here and nothing bad will happen to ________ here* and I didn't know how to tell him that nowhere is safe for his (black) brother so I made him promise to look out for his (black) brother because who else will look out for his (black) brother (with their white privilege) when I'm gone?

When I'm gone my poems will hopefully still be around, and who am I even writing this to? Who are you, (white?) reader, that I feel the need to tell you anything about our (transracial) adoption—a story I can't tell you completely? The one where I say we had a form: "Type of Child Desired," and we checked all the boxes—Caucasian African American Biracial Asian Hispanic Other Racial Mixture and eventually got a document that said, "The Court doth order that the papers be placed in the ended files, indexed in the name of the child, and that they be sealed with an endorsement showing they are not to be opened or inspected except upon permission of this Court."

Which means my (black) son's biological parentage is now a secret only a judge can reveal, the word secret from the Latin verb *secernere*, to sift apart; or *secretus*—an adjective meaning separate (remote / secluded / solitary confidential / intimate). Which means our (black) son's adoption is completely closed, and this was not our choice. His parentage is a secret even from us. Every six months I write a letter to his (black) birthmother and send it to our adoption agency. I only know her first name. I write,

> *Dear ________,*
> *________ is happy, and healthy, and growing quickly.*

She does not know we are white. She did not select us. She let the agency pick, and we were the family next on the list, waiting the longest, probably because we are Jewish. I send snapshots of ________ with the letters, though the (white) social worker told us to be sure the photos only contained our (black) son. In the supermarket line, I'm supposed to say this: *We don't know very much about his birth parents. How have you been? How was your summer?* On the adoption agency training handout, it says responses such as the above can gently educate others, especially if said with a smile. BUT WE ARE ANSWERING PRIMARILY FOR OUR CHILDREN'S EARS.

The all caps are theirs. Our adoption was not a secret, though few people knew about the years of fertility treatments or the match that fell through the year before: the baby we met in the NICU (also black) whose birthmother didn't know she was pregnant—gave birth to her in a college bathroom and then abandoned her (the baby) to the machines and nurses. We held that baby in our (white) arms, dabbed formula from the corners of her mouth until her (black) birthmother decided, weeks later, to return for her. I have never written a poem about this.

When our (black) son was a few weeks old, I found a (white) woman in town who donated her extra breastmilk to me to help feed him because he was having adverse reactions to all the formula we tried. Her brother was adopted from Korea, and she had seen my post in the Human Milk 4 Human Babies—Virginia Facebook Group asking if anyone had extra breastmilk. We'd stand in her kitchen, surrounded by her kids' toys, and she'd place plastic bags—frozen white bricks—in my Styrofoam coolers. Sometimes she'd pour fresh milk, too, from the fridge into the Dr. Brown's bottles I'd brought. I've never written about this either.

I have also never written about the time I took my (black) son to the (black) barbershop in town (New Image) for his first haircut when he was one, and I asked Mr. Johnson (also black) to do a scissor cut, but he pulled out clippers and shaved my (black) son's curls off and while my (black) son was wiggling in my lap and I was trying to keep him still and the clippers buzzed and buzzed I thought this is not what I asked for but I trusted that the (black) barber maybe knew what was better best for my (black) son and I wept when I saw him shorn of his curls—was so flustered I ran out without the small yellow envelope holding locks of my (black) son's hair which Mr. Johnson brought out to the car. I am leaving out the part where my (white) kindergarten son who was waiting in a chair said very loudly to Mr. Johnson *do you know that my brother is African American?* And Mr. Johnson said, *Is that so? Do you know what that means?* and my (white) son got flustered and looked at the floor.

For the past year—including six months during the pandemic—my oldest (white) son has been training for his Bar Mitzvah. He is thirteen now and becomes an adult according to Jewish law once he reads from the Torah. The

Torah is the continuous scroll of parchment on wooden rollers that contains the five books of Moses. Torah scrolls are handwritten by a sofer—a specially trained scribe—on the skin of a kosher animal like a deer, goat, or cow with a turkey quill. Once all the writing in a Sefer Torah has been completed, the sofer sews the pieces of parchment together with thread made of animal veins. A sofer has to know more than 4,000 Judaic laws before beginning a Torah scroll, and the process of writing one scroll can take more than a year. Even a single missing, damaged, or misshapen letter invalidates the entire Sefer Torah, which is considered the holiest object in Judaism. No instrument containing iron or steel or copper can be used in the creation of a Torah scroll, because these metals are used for instruments of war. When Sifrei Torah are damaged or no longer able to be used, they are buried in the ground like the body of a person.

On the first Saturday in June, instead of going to shul for his Bar Mitzvah to read a portion of Numbers from a Torah scroll rescued from Moravia after the Nazis invaded what was then Czechoslovakia, my (white) son spent all morning painstakingly writing the names of every black person who had been killed by police in the last ten years in black sharpie on a rectangle of cardboard he cut from a box, and took it with him when we went to a die-in on Main Street in our small downtown to protest the death of George Floyd—an unarmed black man brutally murdered by police in Minneapolis. My (black) son refused to join me and his (white) brother for the protest. He is seven years old now, and he told us he was afraid he would be killed by the police. For eight minutes and forty-six seconds—the amount of time a Minneapolis police officer pressed his knee on George Floyd's neck—my (white) son and I lay on the asphalt together, in our face masks, surrounded by strangers, our (white) bodies turned toward each other like a set of parentheses.

I Stop Writing the Poem: On Motherhood and the Writing Life

MOLLY SPENCER

When I was in my late twenties, I made a decision: a decision not to be a writer. Although I'd been writing since childhood and once had wanted to make it my profession—or, as I thought of it then and still do, my *life*—I was newly married and I wanted to have children. I sensed that an artistic life would be all-consuming and that motherhood would be all-consuming. I didn't think I could do both, and I chose motherhood.

Even before the first of my three children came along, I set aside my notebooks and books on poetics and craft. Although I mourned for my writing self, for the life that might have been, I believed I'd made the best decision. Being a mother would take the place of being a writer for me, I told myself.

I was wrong, of course.

A few summers ago at a gathering of writers, I heard a poet speak about what he called "the trance." He was referring, he said, to the altered state poets enter when writing. A trance, according to the *Concise Oxford English Dictionary*, is "a half-conscious state characterized by an absence of response to external stimuli." It comes from the Latin *trans*, "across, beyond," and *ire*, "to go." Another writer at that same gathering spoke about the importance of making one's desk a "sanctified space." Sanctified: "set apart or declared holy." Antonym: *profane*: of or related to that which is not sacred; literally "out in front of the temple"; with the moneychangers and the merchants selling doves for ritual sacrifice, sullying a holy place.

In the days and weeks that followed, both of these declarations looped in my mind and I seethed, trying to remember the last time I'd been able to avoid or ignore external stimuli, wishing I had a space set apart for my writing. I thought of waking at four thirty in the morning when my kids were young, slipping downstairs to the kitchen to write, only to have one or more of them wake soon after. I thought of all the times the oven timer or a crying child had interrupted a line of poetry coalescing in my mind, and of the phone calls I'd received from my children at the brief writing retreat I'd attended the previous year: *Where is Dad?* they asked when, at seven o'clock one evening, their father wasn't home from work yet. *When is dinner?* I remembered my guilt when my mother asked, *Are you sure you want to just go away and write? Your family needs you.* I thought of all the mornings or hours or half-hours I'd planned to devote to writing that instead I devoted to fevers, trips to urgent care, dinners for unannounced visits from my in-laws, last-minute repairs to basketball uniforms, skinned knees, wounded little hearts.

And I thought of all the places that had been my writing "desk" over the years: mostly, the end of the kitchen table; once, a card table in my bedroom and then in a corner of the living room; then, in my late thirties, an actual desk, scuffed and handed down from my parents, pushed up to a four-foot section of wall in my kitchen, within reach of the counter on one side and the table on the other. A desk where, yes, I wrote poetry. But also a desk where often a child did homework, where often the laundry sat in baskets waiting to be folded or in stacks waiting to be put away, where most days someone's raincoat, gym bag, hoodie, or all three were slung on the back of my chair. A desk where I paid bills and signed excuse notes and applied band-aids and wiped away tears.

I understood that these declarations—about the trance, about the desk as sacred space—had nothing to do with my life as a writer. They came from another plane of existence that I did not have access to because I am a woman, and women are still responsible for most of the housework, child-rearing, and other care-work in our society. In fact, as Brigid Schulte reported, a recent study found that caregiving fragments women's time so much that, on any given day, a mother has on average ten minutes of uninterrupted leisure time.

Or, as Tess Gallagher puts it in her poem, "I Stop Writing the Poem,"

> No matter who lives
> or who dies, I'm still a woman.
> I'll always have plenty to do.

I don't write in a trance or a sacred space. I write in the orthodontist's waiting room. I write in the car in the ballet studio parking lot. I write in the splinters of time I can find amid my obligations.

I once read an article titled "Emily Dickinson's Handwritten Coconut Cake Recipe Hints at How Baking Figured into Her Creative Process." This about a woman who once wrote in a letter to a friend, "God keep me from what they call households." I was, to put it mildly, skeptical. What actual evidence is there that baking was an important part of Dickinson's process, other than a few lines jotted down on the back of a recipe? How did the author know that scraps of language and ideas for poems didn't follow her everywhere—as they do most writers—and that she didn't write them down wherever she was, on whatever she could find; that she wasn't mid-cake when some words she'd been turning over in her head for months finally arrived as lines of a poem?

What would people think about my creative process, with my desk wedged into a small space in my kitchen? That I found the domestic sphere so inspiring I put my desk between the counter and the kitchen table?

It was a very small house. There was no other place for the desk.

At my desk, I remove a sliver from my daughter's palm. At my desk, I plan next week's meals. At my desk, I answer the phone because it's school calling—my middle son is feverish, please come pick him up.

Having children did not, it ends up, take the place of being a writer for me. In fact, it might be that having children made forgoing the writing life impossible. Perhaps I turned back to writing after my first child was born because I felt torn awake and utterly vulnerable after pushing a defenseless human body out of my own and becoming responsible for its very life. Perhaps it was because he was born just days before the terrorist attacks of September 11, 2001, so horrifically sharpened my perception of the world and our country's place in it.

Perhaps it was because days and months and years of a child—then two, then three—needing care, needing my body, my mind, my daytimes and middle-of-the-nights, the very last shred of my energy and patience, was not enough for me. By which I mean: Although I love my children fiercely and cherish the years I spent at home with them, caregiving work was not fulfilling for me. I mean: Although I would do it all again—chanting nursery rhymes on loop, answering endless questions, wiping down the high chair a thousand-thousand times—I was unhappy.

Amid the labor and the drudgery—and, yes, the occasional magic—of child-rearing, I felt as if the edges of my body were being erased. I missed solitude. I missed the beckoning, empty rooms of my mind. So I started writing again, waking before dawn each morning to get an hour or so of reading and writing in before the kids woke. At that time, I'd have said, "I write," but would not have called myself a writer. Writing was a means of keeping my boundaries intact, of preserving a self amid the obliteration of motherhood.

I write in the margin of my son's crumpled math worksheet left on the floor of the car. I write on a CVS receipt. At the produce market shopping for herbs, I write in the back of my mind.

❧

The danger of the trance is the mythology behind it: that during the trance the writer is a conduit for the Muse. The concept of the Muse comes from the nine daughters of Zeus—the Muses—in Greek mythology, who guarded and apportioned human inspiration and creativity. Throughout history, the practical aspects of women's lives, cultural norms about women's roles, and this mythology, in which the Muse is often eroticized and ardently pursued by the artist, have made the Muse the province of men.

"Sing in me, Muse, and through me tell the story / of that man skilled in all ways of contending," begins Robert Fitzgerald's translation of *The Odyssey*, while Robert Fagles's begins, "Sing to me of the man, Muse, the man of twists and turns." In these lines, invocation is all: the speaker cries out, pleads for a visitation from a goddess-like muse.

Now compare Fagles's and Fitzgerald's language to that of Emily Wilson, the first woman to translate *The Odyssey* in English (and, it's worth noting, a mother): "Tell me about a complicated man. / Muse, tell me how he wandered and was lost." Wilson's simple, direct commands and her plain diction are no-nonsense and conversational: Tell me. There is no crying out, no waiting, no chase, and no plea—just a sense of getting down to business. If a woman's muse exists, it is the muse of Wilson's translation.

I write in the bleachers at the track meet waiting for my son's relay. I write in the car sitting in traffic. I write a line that arrives out of nowhere on the back of my hand.

❧

There came a time in my life when I was very ill and couldn't write—couldn't grip a pen or depress the keys on my laptop keyboard, couldn't even hold a book open because of pain and stiffness in my hands. My whole body hurt. I stopped absorbing nutrients and was anchored to a thick, leaden fatigue. I remember lying on the couch shortly after giving birth to my daughter, child number three. My mom was staying with us because I was too sick to care for the baby or her brothers, then four and two years old. I said to my mom, "I hope I can write again someday." Her reply: "Oh, sweetheart. I just hope you're well enough to take care of your kids someday."

I wished that, too, but I knew that someone else would always take care of my kids if I couldn't. And that no one else could write my poems.

In that moment I felt a little monstrous, but I also understood something for the first time. I understood what my work was: to be a writer. I understood that if I didn't or couldn't do this work, my life would not be *my* life. So perhaps what sent me fiercely and permanently back to writing was the fact of my physical suffering and the death it foreshadowed. It doesn't matter to me now why I returned to writing. That I did is the fundamental fact of my existence.

At my desk I check the children's grades. At my desk I sit and fold towels while my two-year-old nephew stands and folds washcloths: "Corner to corner, Aunt Molly," he says. At my desk I sew ribbons into my daughter's pointe shoes. I prick my finger. It draws blood.

In the Gallagher poem, the speaker has stopped writing the poem in order to fold laundry, and "a small girl / [is] standing next to her mother / watching to see how it's done." The "it" for Gallagher—whose husband died of cancer—may have been how to go on despite grief, but the "it" is also how to live as a woman lives.

Every day, I'm aware that as I pursue my writing life, as I try to juggle writing with my family's needs and my paid work, as I persist in in trying to make something out of nothing in time and in space my life doesn't subside for, my children are watching. I want to show them how it's done. I want them to know that a woman is more than a caregiver. And I want to them to see that a person can do their life's work simply by insisting upon doing it.

It's not easy. To manage it, I live by a mantra: *Do your own work first*. This means a number of things to me: that I spend time every day reading and being attentive to language and (usually) writing; that I devote the best of my mind to writing and give everything else my second-best effort; that I say no to things our culture expects me to say yes to: chaperoning field trips, remembering details from school newsletters, making spaghetti for the team dinner; that I pass on invitations from friends and family; that I put boundaries around the nature and amount of paid work I do so that I have time to write; that, everywhere and every day, I preserve a province of my mind for poetry. This has sometimes caused tension in my relationships, close and not-so-close. Why? Because the culture doesn't approve of a woman who puts her own work first: would call her selfish; would say her priorities are out of order.

I write at the sink washing dishes. I write chopping onions. I write with a baby on one hip, stirring dinner on the stove, as if my life depends on it. Because it does.

❧

I'm reading an interview in which a male poet—one whose work I admire greatly, one whom I consider a friend—said that writing poems is "impossible."

I want to spit.

Later, same day, I come across a quote attributed to Leo Tolstoy: "One ought only to write when one leaves a piece of one's flesh in the inkpot, each time one dips one's pen."

Fuck that. I say it out loud. Fuck the trance, the sacred space, the "impossibility" of writing poems, the ridiculously high stakes: flesh in the ink pot.

I write in the car wash. I write in the furnace room of my parents' basement, early on Thanksgiving morning, before it's time to make the pies. I write in the surgery waiting room, watching the clock, waiting for the doctors to come out and say it was much more complicated than they thought it would be, but my son is going to be fine.

❧

Today it hurts to write—actually hurts—because I cut my finger badly slicing bread. I take a look and see the deep red gap, flesh pulling back, and I know I should have it stitched. But I'm babysitting my feverish nephew. My son has a doctor's appointment at three, and I have to take my daughter and three other Girl Scouts to a campground in the Santa Cruz Mountains at five. I can't miss the window—the road in and out is one way: in from five to six only; out after six.

So the kitchen—not the inkpot, or the page—is where I leave my flesh, just a bit on the blade of a knife. I rinse the knife and bandage my hand. I put my nephew down for a nap and walk to my desk. With my foot, I push a laundry basket away from the chair. I move the piles of bills and school forms to the side. And, waiting for nothing and no one, in the twenty minutes before the kids get home from school, I write a poem. Which is not impossible.

I write on the back, inside cover of the book I'm reading while my son gets a post-op ultrasound. I write while the chicken roasts. I write one word in the next blank space of my notebook. Then I write another.

❧

If we make writing into something that requires waiting for a half-conscious state to occur in a space set apart and holy, we miss out on the kind of art made in the messy, material, fragmented, actual, ten-minutes-at-a-time world where we live. We also devalue, if not exclude, from our concept of what makes a "writer" those who don't have time to wait for a trance, who don't have space in their homes or their lives for writing, let alone a sanctified space.

And make no mistake, the people who get excluded have been and will be women—the caretakers of children, the elderly, and their neighbors; the ones who do the most housework at home and "housekeeping" tasks at work; the ones who are paid less for the same work as their male counterparts. And they have been and will be especially women of color, who face all of these obstacles, compounded by systemic and individual racism that creates even more roadblocks to a creative life.

I'll be plain: If you have a family *and* have time to wait for the trance *and* have a physical space that you can cordon off from the rest of your life and sanctify, you are probably a man whose partner does most of the care-work. And there's a good chance you're a white man, for whom and by whom the world of creative work—and the world of all work, really—was designed.

Every day, I write whatever I can wrestle from my mind and from language, reading and listening, putting words down on the page. Often in a slender crack of time between obligations. With my simple materials: pen, paper. Despite interruptions. At my scuffed and cluttered desk that I have dragged back and forth across the country, following my husband's jobs. Where I write poems and checks and essays and appointment reminders and book reviews and grocery lists. In a room in a house where a family lives. Apart from that which is sacred. I read and listen and write: a word, a list of words, a line, a couplet. Sometimes a whole draft, listened for, attended to, worked at, returned to. I have written lines and poems and whole manuscripts of poems; essays; criticism; and a graduate critical thesis in exactly this way. Or, as Sarah Vap puts it in *Winter: Effulgences*, her gorgeous and wrenching meditation on—among other things—interruption: my work "has sputtered out of holes, across many years, during which I was interrupted every few seconds, I. / Good morning love. Come here."

And, yes, very occasionally, a poem—or part of a poem or most of a poem—arrives as if from a realm beyond, and I feel very nearly entranced, very nearly holy. And these times are as rare as when the baby sleeps through one night after months or years of not. Are like the five minutes every six months during which there is no dirty laundry in the hamper and no one is hungry. Are like the one week every other year during which no child gets sick or hurt. But these moments are not how to write poems or books of poems. They are not how to have a writing life, especially if you are a woman or a mother.

Rather than wait for the trance or a sacred space, I hope writers will do their own work first. I hope they will labor—a word that scholars think may have derived from the Latin *labere*, "to totter," in the sense of tottering under a burden—rather than wait for inspiration. I hope they will say no to whatever they have to in order to do their life's work. I hope they will write, not in the absence of obstacles, but in the pits and gullies around and through them. Not from inspiration in the language of the Muse, but from their daily lives in the language of stovetops and bodies and brooms and blood. And interruptions.

At my desk, I cut the tags from my son's pajamas so I can wash them and take them to the hospital during visiting hours tonight. At my desk, I check my bank account. At my desk, I sign the decree formalizing my divorce.

Years later, another house, the hush and brittle dark of winter before dawn. It's six. I'm writing at my profane desk shoved into the corner of my bedroom, piled with stacks of essays I need to grade and bills that need paying, with the hum and clink of the kids eating breakfast in the background, in the midst of my actual life. My daughter taps lightly on my door, which is always ajar. She needs help with her homework.

I say, "Good morning, sweetheart. Of course I'll help you."

I stop writing the poem.

Writing Prompts

The prompts in this part take up themes of the bodily and the cerebral in various ways. Some invite you to bring the body into your writing, and others develop your understanding of the form of the poem and how line breaks and other formal decisions can shape a poem's meaning or impact on its reader.

1) The poems in this part use different formal techniques, including couplets, or two-line stanzas, sections, and prose poems. Find a bit of freewriting from an earlier prompt and play around with putting it in different forms. How does the poem feel different in couplets than when it's all in one stanza? How do very short lines work differently than long lines?
2) Beth Ann Fennelly, Carolina Ebeid, and Hope Wabuke all use sections in their poems. For Fennelly, these sections allow movement through time, from her daughter's first weeks through the end of the first year and weaning. Ebeid's poem uses titled sections to consider different aspects of her son's childhood and autism diagnosis. In Wabuke's poem, sections allow her to switch between different modes, moving from contemplation to description to questions and back. Write a poem that uses sections.
3) Many poems in this part use surprising metaphors to consider how the body is transformed by pregnancy and birth. In "Latching On, Falling Off," Beth Ann Fennelly celebrates nursing, writing, "Once, I bared my chest / and found an animal. Once, I was delicious." Kendra DeColo's "I Pump Milk like a Boss" takes a different tack, showing the nurs-

ing mother out in the world and having to hand-express milk on the side of the road and in a bar's bathroom sink, among other unexpected places. In Alexa Doran's "C-Section," the speaker addresses her son, saying that at his birth he was a "Cloud ladled out of me" and later adding that he "rose like any rainbow." Pick a moment and develop an unexpected comparison. If it helps, you could borrow DeColo's structure of repeated comparisons; instead of pumping milk like a boss, you could employ another action and a different comparison.

4) The form of Khadijah Queen's "Terrell Owens Private Messaged Me" is a single, breathless sentence structured almost like a joke working toward a punchline. Using this poem as a model, relate an anecdote about parenting that ends with a surprise. You may want to try using the prose poem form and to write it as a single sentence using only "&" to connect each moment.

5) Shamala Gallagher's "Final Neon" consists primarily of a series of images, including a bag of candy bought at a gas station, the "city at the world's end," and "the belly-child kicking," and concludes with a final pronouncement: "I don't want a drink." Write a poem in which you describe the world around you at a pivotal moment and avoid disclosing what you're really thinking about until the final line.

In the World

WRITER ELIZABETH STONE'S STATEMENT ABOUT the "momentous" decision to have a child—"it is to decide forever to have your heart go walking around outside your body"—gained viral recognition with the advent of the internet in the late 1990s, and it has since been quoted and misquoted and attributed to people ranging from Steve Jobs to Hillary Clinton. The statement resonates with us. It can be terrifying and exhilarating to send a child into the world. In this part, poets and essayists grapple with what it means to expose their children to the world in its violence, senselessness, and indifference, to the world in its astonishing beauty and joy.

Current and historical events serve as the backdrop to many of these pieces. Nicole Cooley's "Homeland Security" takes place shortly after the terrorist attacks of September 11, 2001. Emmy Pérez, who lives and works on the U.S.–Mexico border, uses the words of former U.S. attorney general Jeff Sessions in "Cajas/ Boxes with Zero Tolerance #9" to decry the U.S. policy of separating undocumented parents from their children. In her essay, she discusses the weight and ethics of writing about the traumas on the border. In her poem "War Stories" and her essay "Savage Flower: One Mother Writing War," Pamela Hart weighs the responsibilities of a mother of a soldier deployed in Afghanistan in what has come to be called the "Endless War." Natalie Shapero considers birthing a child into the same world that allowed the Holocaust, noting in "Monster" that "my greatest fear // is the ongoing nature of history."

What does it mean to bring a child into a culture steeped in racism, sexism, homophobia, illness, and inequality, onto a planet on the brink of environmental collapse? Joy Katz, Erika Meitner, and Tina Chang consider the ways in which their race and their children's race positions them. Lisa L. Moore writes of avoiding states where her children's other mother is a "legal stranger." Sara Mumolo's "10 weeks and intermittent: earning" considers the care of a newborn alongside a partner's return to work at two weeks and the speaker's own return to work, driven both by the need to "earn" and by the difficulty of navigating benefits at her workplace. In "Suicide Prevention" Sarah Blake realizes, "I don't know how to talk to him about death."

The encounter with the world frequently feels bleak, but these writers also find hope and connection. Poets Aimee Nezhukumatathil, Clarissa Mendiola, and January Gill O'Neil find beauty and solace in nature. Both Shara Lessley and Chanda Feldman find mentors and hope in the world in the form of other writers. It is all the world and all of history, Tina Chang reminds us in "Revolutionary Kiss," that leads to the moment of a child's creation.

I Could Be a Whale Shark

AIMEE NEZHUKUMATATHIL

Bolinao, Philippines

I am worried about tentacles.
How you can still get stung
even if the jelly arm disconnects
from the bell. My husband
swims without me—farther
out to sea than I would like,
buoyed by salt and rind of kelp.
I am worried if I step too far
into the China Sea, my baby
will slow the beautiful kicks
he has just begun since we landed.
The *quickening*, they call it,
but all I am is slow, a moon jelly
floating like a bag in the sea.
Or a whale shark. Yes—I could be
a whale shark, newly spotted
with moles from the pregnancy—
my wide mouth always open
to eat and eat with a look that says
Surprise! Did I eat that much?
When I sleep, I am a flutefish,
just lying there, swaying back
and forth among the kelpy mess
of sheets. You can see the wet
of my dark eye awake, awake.
My husband is a pale blur
near the horizon, full of adobo
and not waiting thirty minutes
before swimming. He is free
and waves at me as he backstrokes
past. This is how he prepares
for fatherhood. Such tenderness
still lingers in the air: the Roman
poet Virgil gave his pet fly

the most lavish funeral, complete
with meat feast and barrels
of oaky wine. You can never know
where or why you hear
a humming on this soft earth.

The Experiment

ALISON STINE

The first time we collected hen of the woods,
I wondered if they would kill me. No reply.

They were delicious, bright as hunter's caps,
squeaky meat. How long does it take, I thought

at each sponge-full. I thought, had my nails
turned blue? I was scared by my child. I was left

by his father. Left over and over in the way
men leave before leaving, each affair a little

practice, each abuse a little closer out the door
to *I can't*... But I could. For a long time. There is a theory

that pain carries down from generations. Trauma
will out. A scientist I knew shook

pregnant mice in a tube, then measured
how, months later, the babies ran. This was a boy

who loved boys and also me. He photographed
me smoking a cigar. I wish I had that shot.

He told me he was afraid of men, but later,
married one. Sometimes I think what happened to us

didn't really happen to us. Not to our bones,
but to our blood. Now my lover knows

the dog breathing, my wild mud pupils
that relax in the spring trap of a hand,

brows like a hill road. My body is a doorway
through which pain may pass. My blood holds

the mothers, all of the girls of the yard, girls
of the trees, girls of the closed doors. Girls in jail.

The experiment was to traumatize the mothers.
The trees had no answer. The world

held no reference. I ate to find out would I die.

This Year the Role of Boiling Hail Will Be Played by ______________

MAGGIE SMITH

My four-year-old son says God
made the planets. Even Mars.
Yeah, God's in space, he says.

This is the same boy who played
the boiling hail in his preschool
Passover play, each child a plague.

I took pictures: his tee shirt covered
with taped-on red streamers
and small white balloons.

Some people believe in plagues,
I'd told him. Some people believe
that God set each planet in place,

each moon and star. Can't you
just see Him with His tweezers
and jeweler's eye, muttering

under His breath and painstakingly
affixing? Some people believe
He set you here, I say. Set me.

That there are no mistakes.
Some people believe that.
I believe it, he says.

Homeland Security

NICOLE COOLEY

Write against narrative: here is the television's blue
square of light, milk needling my skin.

The September sky burns metal blue, each day's fabric
torn away from my window.

The television's stark horizontal. The city dimmed,
asphalt shaking with the subway's rush toward home.

Write toward the girl, asleep beside me, her body
made of mine.

The television's expanse of glass, its flat metallic voice,
its slur of headlines.

I hold the baby while jets cross and recross over this city.

The current threat advisory is—

Write against blankness, a sheet strung tight,
a bed the color of ash: white, white, white.

10 weeks and intermittent: earning

SARA MUMOLO

The Owh cry—head, hands, feet—a muslin series of folds with living inside. You install the light dimmer, so I can see to feed, fold. You teach me to swaddle before you go back to work at two weeks. You go, and I don't understand until years later. Tuck the corners in tight. I call to get more time off, but I don't get how the benefits work. Neither does the voice asking me to return. At ten weeks go. Not a petal on the black bough. Verbs. I can't yet walk up the hill to our apartment. I go. I fold. My work has benefits. You move furniture from one house to the next, up flights, through the woods, to the beach. You move you move you drive you move you lift. You fall asleep on the train and don't make it home. You save your coworker P's life in back of the work truck in Orinda. Blue face, CPR, ambulance. Not too far away I'm at the work desk. It wasn't oxy; it was fentanyl. You don't make it home. Four years later P goes missing for weeks. You stay up until light learning code on a TV screen. Computer hums, revs while M and I sleep. You back the 32-foot truck into a Porsche. You pay the ticket. You dream you kill someone and tell me days later when you finally realize it's not real. Hunger wakes us. I read about the Neh cry on the held screen, a glow by which I see the feed.

The Average Mother Now Spends Twice as Many Hours on Childcare as Did Her Counterpart in 1965, and She Also Spends Three Times as Many Hours Working Outside the Home; or, How to Sing a Song of Sixpence When You're Really Feeling Wry

CAMILLE T. DUNGY

We flew through a thunderstorm on our way into
Pittsburgh, landing without incident, but a hailstorm
            descended, delaying our bags.
                        Forty minutes.
                One hour.

When we got into the Town Car, both the driver and his
    wife's well-timed pot roast were burning.

When he started driving, the baby started screaming.

        She wouldn't stop screaming.

The label peeking from below the driver's cap left a red mark
    on his scalp. We were the worst people
                        he had ever known.

Pittsburgh, late April. Cold as we drove past industrial parks
    outside the city. Cold as the setting sun burnished mirrored
buildings bronze.

        She wouldn't stop crying.

I leaned over her car seat. Said, *Every person in this car is*
    upset right now, but you are the only one screaming.

We drove out of some sort of tunnel, everyone quiet now,
    smiling, over the yellow bridges into Pittsburgh.

Suicide Prevention

SARAH BLAKE

New signs at all the local train stations—
Suicide Prevention Lifeline.

I'm glad my son can't read yet.

Yesterday morning he made up a friend, Lofty,
who was captured by bad guys.

My husband asked, *Loffy?*

He said, *No, with a T.*
If it was a V, it would be Lof-vee.
He's starting to get it.

If it was a circle, it would be Lof-circle.
He's almost starting to get it.

Today he tells me he's dead. He's a ghost.
He misses his ghost family.
Something's wrong because they're inside
the wall but he can't get through.

Then he walks into the wall to show me.

Then a ghost ladybug shows up who can get
through the wall, and he saves everyone.

My son bends down to hug a family
of very small ghosts.

I don't know how to talk to him about death.

When I told him about his great grandfather,
who he's named after, and that conversation
led right where you think—*He's dead*—

he told me, *Only bad guys die*, and I
could only argue that so many times.

Before I tell my son about suicide, I want to
tell him about murder, I want to tell him
about dying of an illness, about dying in sleep.

It feels awful to hold that plan inside me,
to know this ranking of death.

Do I tell him about genocide last? Or
how you keep hearing for a few minutes
after you die? How I'd like him to play me
a nice song and repeat that he loves me.

How he better tell me first
if he wants to take his life because
I would understand that.

I've understood that for a long time.

Monster

NATALIE SHAPERO

1.

Eight women in this class, and me the lone

one refusing to say which name I've chosen.
Isn't anyone else convinced of curses?
And regarding being asked to state my greatest

fear about having a baby, it has of course
to do with one of the outfits I have been gifted,
snap-around swaddle all crammed

with dull-colored rabbits, except for one rabbit

that's speeding-ticket red. Why just one?
I would have to be a monster

2.

not to be put in mind of *Schindler's List*,
which is filmed of course in black and white,

except for the one red jacket worn by a child
in the Warsaw Ghetto, then later seen draped
on a pushcart laden with bodies. My greatest fear

is the ongoing nature of history,

its verve and predation and oceanic rage. Or am I
supposed to fixate on something smaller? I recall
with ill feeling the curator, viewing a meager

tribute with disdain: CAN'T CALL YOURSELF A HOLOCAUST
MEMORIAL UNTIL YOU HAVE A TRAIN.

In Defense of the Empty Chaos Required for Adequate Preparation

ERIKA MEITNER

June 16, 2017

When the (white) man at the pool says
my (black) son reminds him of his youngest and asks
how old is he, eight? I say, *no, four* and I am not
flattered but terrified of the implications because
in study after study the average age overestimation

for black boys exceeded four years, because black boys
are viewed as adults by white undergraduates white
police officers white suburban residents at the age of
ten they lose the protection afforded to them by
assumed childhood innocence ten ten ten my older

(white) son is ten and still struggles to tie his shoes
sometimes curses loves Minecraft and cheese and
catching newts was not sent home from Nature Camp
this week for writing *Snoop Dog* and *Smoke Pot* on
his newspaper craft project but the director spoke

with me at pickup and we laughed and he said *I didn't
do stuff like that until eighth grade* and I was still mortified
that this (white) biologist thought I was maybe a terrible
(white) mother (white) pothead (white) something
so when I call home to see what else we need at Target

I am always calling home from the aisles of [insert
store here there is always something we need] and
Steve says *get extra water guns—they're all broken—
the kids like the ones with pump action best*
and though they have bright orange safety tips

and though they look nothing like actual firearms
with their Nerf logo stamped on the side and their
white and blue and green neon plastic I hesitate

I stand in the aisle staring at the Super Soaker
package with the giant wave and the white boy

on the front aiming his hands his gun straight at me
I stand and stand in the aisle I can't help it
(Microburst2 Blasts up to 33 feet / Also look for
Freezefire BottleBlitz / Do not aim at eyes or face /
TO AVOID INJURY: Use only clean tap water)

To avoid injury to avoid unconscious dehumanization to make sure you see my son as a person
to make sure you see my son as a child he is four
he is not eight he is four he is big for his age yes
he is not likely to bring violence to your neighborhood

the study describes use of force as takedown or
wrist lock as kicking or punching as striking with
a blunt object as using a police dog or restraints
or hobbling as using tear gas or electric shock
or killing on the radio the cop who shot Philando

Castile is found not guilty his girlfriend's child
who was in the back seat when he was shot
who was four years old then is named Dae'Anna
and you can hear her on the tape after Philando
is shot after her (black) mother is down on her knees

in handcuffs you can hear the (black) child saying
It's ok mommy . . . it's ok, I'm right here with you
she is tender with her mother preternaturally
calm she is four and only dehumanization not
police officers' prejudice against blacks—conscious

or not—was linked to violent encounters with black
children in custody according to the study

Raising White Men II

LISA L. MOORE

Mimi

is what my children call me

nobody wanted us to have these babies

I broke it to my parents like bad news

let a thousand flowers bloom is nice in theory

my dyke friend hissed in disappointment

we don't drive across Oklahoma

where their other mother is just another

legal stranger, dangerous, confused

and criminal

our children call her

Mama

Cajas/Boxes with Zero Tolerance #9

EMMY PÉREZ

> They are the ones who broke the law, they
> are the ones who endangered their own
> children on their trek. The United States,
> on the other hand, goes to extraordinary
> lengths to protect them while the parents
> go through a short detention period.
>
> —Jeff Sessions

They are the ones who were told their children
were taken to bathe—and not returned. They

are the ones whose nursing babies and toddlers
were forced to wean and left in wet diapers.

And their other young ones also cried
for mami, for papá, for tía, for ______

and were told they were an *orchestra* without
a conductor. And enough in this country

elected the conductor with his fist
in the air, without music, without ocean,

without moon, without the very earth. He
was the one and she another and he yet

another who said they'd be taking her child
the next day and said "Happy Mother's Day."

My Daughter Returns from My Ex-Wife's House with Braids in Her Hair

ALLISON BLEVINS

Another woman's twists undo themselves
between my fingers. I become like silence,
caught in the gaps. In the slow shadow of evening,
my daughter and I relearn each other
after our night as separate bodies. Her breath and fingers sneak
into my clothes. I mouth into her fleshy crooks.

My daughter's hair, kinked by some other woman, slips
wild down her back, gallops after her down the hall.
We laugh like insomniacs.

A Short Prose Piece on One of the Book's Central Themes

JULIE CARR

We are raking leaves. Or I am raking leaves and she is wandering around picking up leaves, and a man shows up. He looks hot, I mean he looks overheated and sunburned or, the red face of an alcoholic, and I know when he calls me "ma'am" that he wants something. The usual "your neighbor told me to ask you," then shows his hand, the infected gash. I remember this from subways, the men with amputations exposed or diseased faces or wounded legs—he shows his hand and begins to speak. I'm standing still, not saying no not saying yes, I'm listening, and she walks toward him and holds out a leaf, which he takes, then she takes it back. He laughs a bit uncomfortably, and continues: the wife who left him, the kid at home, and how he had a Band-Aid but sweated it off, how he used to bring in two thousand a week, but now zero, and he lifts his hat to show the other wound, not so bad as the one on his hand, more a scrape or a bruise on the forehead, and then, almost in slow motion, still standing before him, she opens her arms and wraps them around his legs, her face too close to his crotch. I, also slow, say Lucy, come here, and he pats her on the back and says, aren't you affectionate. I take her hand and we go inside to find money, a ten is what I have, and I return and give it to him. Then he leaves, not without first offering to bring her his son's toys, since his wife left with his son. I say no, thank you, you don't know, he says, how awful this is to have to ask for work this way, and I say I'm sorry, and have a good day, which feels stupid. We are raking, there is silence, and I say, why did you hug him? I don't know, she says. I say, if Mommy and Daddy are not there, then don't hug a stranger, ok? but if we are and we say it's ok, it's ok. There is another silence. Then she says, don't ever say that again.

Nearly There

CLARISSA MENDIOLA

For a moment, we are home.
Saltwater etches a crude map
across the hull of your back
charting a path to your tiny center.
This is a brown child's topography—
sand clings to your ankles
like so many freckles to prove
your relation to the sun. You whisper
Mommy, we are brown because
we come from an island.
I pause to revel in the words,
how they land on your heart,
how they enter the world again in song.
Sweetie, we've been floating
our entire lives, I say, and here were are,
grounded, up to our shoulders in ocean.
It's a familiar pleasure, we almost grasp it
with our sea sticky fingers if not
for the heap of spondylus fragments
in our palms. If we let go, we could leave
a trail for others lost at sea.
I sink my hands into hot sand and watch
you walk toward the water,
your knowing stride, your sun
darkened arms an outrigger,
your hair catching the wind
a pandanus sail.

from "The Color Cure"

JOY KATZ

We were six families who brought names with us to Vietnam. These names we brought with us to name the babies were an invasive species that clung to our luggage and strollers and footsoles.

Some of us thought ourselves saviors. Some of us shut ourselves in hostels with white American names. To cover the babies, we brought with us white American names. The names were so big they split the seams of silk áo dàis.

Grandmothers threw handkerchiefs over us, they said "keep the babies out of the sun." We tracked ourselves through alleys and clinics and embassies and rice fields and crab nets. We carried the babies against our chests, in sweat. What passed through our damp shirts to their faces was the names.

If blood in a poem could link us up, as I am called up by blood to bless the Torah—called as *daughter of*:

בתיה אלקהא בת חייה-שרה ודניאל דוב

Instead, someone with a clipboard called my name and I was handed a son. I remember the clipboard. A son was handed to me through the air. I was handed a glass of water and then a son. An Australian medic put the baby on a scale and said "they are not all so handsome." *They*. I remember the water glass was striped. How light was that boy in my arms? I don't remember. I remember ants in the half-sandwich I had left in the car.

How you know you are ~~not~~ a Vietnamese mother

You ~~do not~~ forget to keep the baby out of the sun

You are ~~not~~ beautiful enough

~~Not~~ are you beautiful

Enough.

"Do they give infants milk in Vietnam? I bet not"

How do you know ~~you are~~ you are not a Vietnamese mother

~~What is it you must~~ tell him of the world

~~That there is~~ a woman he came from

~~What is it you are afraid to~~ tell him

~~that she loves him~~

You do not ~~should~~ know

~~Remember~~ the right song to sing the baby

He ~~would not have~~ dug his nails into ~~his birth mother~~ my arm till it bled

You are ~~let yourself go~~ careless

Look at your sun-stained arms

~~You forget~~ you bring him to Huong so she can teach him ~~teach us~~ Vietnamese

Teach us ~~him~~

how to know you are ~~not his~~ right ~~Vietnamese~~ mother

~~You checked~~ that box was checked for me

by grandmothers who threw napkins over us in sun

Keep the boy white they said *by any means*

Whiteness hides inside the names that live in the stories I make up. *Once upon a time there was a boy and the boy's name was . . .*—why not: Hykeem, Montray, Tariq. Having reached into a jewel case and stolen this name, Tariq, the edge of my hand is stuck with jags of broken glass. Is how my son looks at me when I say, *Tariq*.

❧

Even with 50 SPF, my son gets more and more dark at swim camp. In Vietnam, this is not done. However mothers (meaning Vietnamese mothers, of which I was entrusted to be one) can keep our children's skin light, to that we are bound.

In just hours his skin deepens, his eyes a crease in this new version of his face.

He comes off the camp bus and his color resembles the oiled leather wallet my father kept on top of his dresser at night. At the base of his back, a kingly blue gleam.

I am visiting a friend on the opposite coast. My cell buzzes. On the backlit screen, a black boy—whose child in this familiar shirt?

Flash of strangeness, a spill I am bound to contain.

❧

Lieutenant Colonel Gilbert Krom, my uncle-in-law, served in Korea, Germany, Vietnam. After retiring, Gil traced his line of the family back to the 1600s in New York (Ulster County).

When we adopt our son, Gil's gift to us is a printout of the genealogy. On the left side, an endless column of Dutch names. Opposite, on the right, under our boy's Vietnamese name, none. Three hundred years of Kroms unroll across the floor, alongside a blazing, blank, invisible Asian clan.

Before I walked down the aisle, before anyone I love was alive, before I was born, did these two families intersect? In other words is there a bullet hole on the timeline across from Gil's platoon in Vietnam? If there were any Kroms left, I would explain to them why I am keeping that in my poem.

War Stories

PAMELA HART

Stories of war begin midsentence is one way to start. This isn't a story of war. This is the mother on the idea of the son at war. Can he kill is a story. Will the mother blame herself could be another. And how does the mother feel. The mother doesn't like that word. The mother likes the word think. Will ideas versus feelings get in the way. Is this the story of mothers of soldiers. The mothers' lives are windy. The air is elastic. The story is a story on the idea of war and the son who might kill or be killed. She could or could not change this.

Revolutionary Kiss

TINA CHANG

I had never created man before so I invented my son first as a dream body. In order to create the dream body I must first believe in the force of opposites, a terrible tension of what has existed and the struggle yet to come. And it is true, that I had a notion of him for many years; for generations my imagination traveled in search of him.

It seems unlikely that a kiss would have roots in the Haitian Revolution, but it does. Over a century ago, an uprising of hundreds of thousands of slaves freed themselves from chain and rope, from whip and guillotine, from bondage through the struggle of blood. They fought for thirteen years in a revolution to stand on the shores of their own land, newly named Haiti, as free people and they kissed the ground however damp with the blood of their mothers, fathers, brothers, and sons. Slaves, newly liberated, whispered my son's name, his body envisioned there, beneath the rust of shackles, beside shards of slaveowners' homes, rising with smoke from burned plantations. Past the pinnacle of scoured light, past the canopy of trees dripping with the uprising of future leaves, my son begins his journey to me.

Once there was a chain of kisses as my mother said goodbye to her brothers and sisters lined in a row, as she left Taiwan for America, a shock of leis around her neck as she waved to a country of ghosts. Her history was equally complex. She left China in 1949, before communists led by Chairman Mao took over mainland China. My mother crowded into a boat that would take her to the coast of Taiwan known as *the beautiful island*, which she would one day yearn to leave.

By foot, by boat, by train, by bus, by plane. It seems impossible these two histories intertwine so that one day I may find a dream body housed inside mine. All along, I wring my hands and worry, will I know how to mother him? What language will I speak? What will my mother utter once she discovers the detour of my ancestry? Will she abandon me, turn the portraits of my ancestors toward the wall, backs directed away from my longing?

When I woke, the doctor's voice was muffled and thick. My mind moved in syncopated pulses and I pushed until all energy drained and my body cracked open. Liquid gold rushed away. Finally and now. He arrived, a purpled creature, violet and squirming, face crushed into an emperor's expression.

Born from the urgency of immigrants, how futile all of my years of worrying. I should have known my boy would row his small boat to me, regardless of the sky above that shook down its lightning, and even if the ground was bruised and famished of fruit and even freedom, he would continue on as if a force were lulling him to bedrock. Right here between his eyebrows, there is swell of light, a country where I belong, no longer a stranger to my own skin. My mouth to his temple, an alarm cries. Tanks roll through the tale squeaking, turning their heavy wheels. When I kiss him, history's weapons fall from my pockets, shields cast beneath attalea trees. I will now end my days of resistance, my lips searching the entirety of his dream face made mortal, my lost shadows now migrating in unison.

Maybe the Milky Way

JANUARY GILL O'NEIL

My son fills the inner space between my arm and body.
We lay in the wet grass in the heart of the White Mountains,

far from the glare of city lights. *Maybe it's the Milky Way.*
Orion's belt drifts in a hemisphere so crowded with stars

we cannot locate it. We laugh, finger fine clusters of yellow-white
to create spirographs in star fields, our empty hands outstretched

and hungry—for what? We do not know. Like a private tour
of a planetarium's dome, it is our night. We know the stars

are watching us, would cast our shadows into the next galaxy
if they could. They watch him as I watch him, light reflecting light,

his beauty too dangerous to touch or hold or explain.
The love for my son would incinerate us if I get too close.

Tonight our hands girdle the heavens as we write new names
for ourselves, wishing on stars that neither shoot nor fall,

dissolve into stardust, while the campfire smolders
and the marshmallows, unattended, burn orange to black.

“Estranged, Changed, Suspended”: My Path to Plath

SHARA LESSLEY

We must have hiked five miles that day after starting down the road to Hardcastle Crags in morning rain. At Gibson Mill, we split a piece of carrot cake, warmed our bellies with tea. Behind a building run by the National Trust, school children skimmed the pond, dragged up muck in nets then dumped their hauls into white plastic tubs for inspection. For a few minutes, we stopped to watch them before veering off toward what was once a packhorse trail, my six-year-old calling out *oak*, *pine*, *beech*, and other trees he’d been studying in a guidebook. As we moved deeper into the ravine, we spotted heron, dippers, woodpeckers, common songbirds, small brown things chattering in the brush. But the crags themselves (hiking up to and around them at least) were harder to see—shrouded in vegetation, a few rough caps of rock jutting out from the foliage. Not at all what I expected. “We came over the moor-top,” writes Sylvia Plath in her Yorkshire poem, “The Great Carbuncle,” “Through air streaming and green-lit / Stone farms foundering in it”—and, indeed, we did, crisscrossing the footpaths, stopping to photograph mushrooms that sprouted from the faces of deadwood. The children laughed, sang songs, complained as afternoon gave way and their legs fatigued. Squatting near a brook in my wellies while the kids rested, I thought about Plath catching her reflection in similarly clear water, and then strained to see the strange figure, which was my own self, looking back at me—another expat, wife, ghostly mother.

The years we lived in England, I embedded a series of literary excursions within family holidays. Just three and four when we moved to Oxford, our children were agreeable and eager to explore. Had anyone asked whether I’d marry, move overseas, or have kids; whether I’d book a cottage in the northern moorlands in order to more fully immerse myself in Sylvia Plath’s poetry—I would have thought them a little mad. Still, after nine years of dating, my husband and I exchanged vows. In Amman, Jordan, I gave birth to a son and a daughter. And, after a decade of dismissing Plath as a poetic influence, I made a pilgrimage to the stony village of Heptonstall where I scrambled the packed walkway of collapsed headstones littered across the Old

Church's thirteenth-century courtyard. Although the rain gave way, the grey grit-stone dripped, and I stopped to watch a woman sketching the mossy archways and ruined bell-tower. In the chantry of the adjacent church, St. Thomas the Apostle, a cellist rehearsed for a weekend concert. I remember thinking that the whole scene seemed both ordinary and overly poetic. I eavesdropped for several minutes, then made my way to the nearby cemetery where, in February 1963, after gassing herself in the kitchen of her flat on Primrose Hill, Sylvia Plath was buried.

I'm not a rabid Plath fan. I don't count myself among the activists happy to scratch the poet's married name, Hughes, from her headstone. I didn't leave a trinket or note. The truth is that my journey to Yorkshire, much like Plath's, was an unlikely one that initially stemmed from a sense of obligation. I first read *Ariel* in the late 1990s in an effort to hit the marks I believed an aspiring writer should. Having paid my respects, I went on to dutifully purchase *The Unabridged Journals* and *The Bell Jar*. Like many English majors, I'd been assigned a spattering of Plath's poems: "The Colossus," "Lady Lazarus," "Daddy." I didn't like her. Or, rather, I didn't like how she mirrored the things I feared being labeled (*By whom?* I now ask with amusement)—meaning theatrical, pushy, ambitious, driven by self-victimization, too eager to please. Having bought into the archetype early, for years I failed to see Plath's work with real depth or sensitivity. I hadn't internalized the poems, in other words, but the myth behind their making; which is to say, the reductive framing of Plath as either conniving ingénue or tragic martyr. And so, while I occasionally read her in graduate school, Plath became little more than a cautionary example of the risks of self-exhibitionism and dramatization, as well as of what to avoid in both cadence and tone.

An Irish diplomat's daughter taken to England when she was just six, the poet Eavan Boland knew something of long bitter British winters, especially from the perspective of outsider. I suspect this is partly why she was sensitive to Plath's plight as the mother of young children during the notorious season of early 1963 when, all across the country, pipes iced, trains froze to the tracks, snow collapsed power stations and roofs, electricity failed and, with it, indoor heat. And so, hearing Boland frame Plath's late work within this context, hearing her describe how the thirty-year-old Plath would rise at 4 a.m. to write what would become the best poems of her life—well, to hear it, from another mother-poet's perspective was something. Or was something to me when, the fall after I finished my MFA and arrived at Stanford University, I heard her characterize what Plath was up against as she drafted the lines animating the "red / Shred" in the little boy's fist at the end of "Balloons." "That a young poet-mother . . . with her baby boy and the clear-eyed dark had enough leverage to shift an ancient conversation should not be a surprise," observed Boland of the tonal evolution in Plath's later work. What Plath faced in her last living months wasn't only bad weather (as Boland's insights revealed), but a deeper "spiritual winter." Far from the country that birthed her and by that time estranged from her husband, Plath was very much alone. Which raises the question: what was left of the poet's notion of "home"—except, perhaps, her writing and children? It's no wonder, then, that the two fused together. "In this poem a mother nurses her baby son by candlelight," reflects Plath in her last recorded interview for the BBC, "and finds in him a beauty which, while it may not ward off the world's ill, does redeem her share of it."

A year before I began studying with Eavan Boland at Stanford, I memorized "Morning Song" (the first poem I recited to my son just after his birth in Amman). Although suspicious of Plath, I was astonished by the fact of "Morning Song"—its seeming inevitability and imaginative leaps, its pacing and dark humor. Mostly, I loved how entire worlds spilled out from six stanzas whose plot might be summarized in three words: a baby cries. *A baby cries*—that's it! And yet that cry holds, at least by implication, the speaker's personal history, our shared human history, the history of creation, natural history, the celestial. "Love set you going like a fat gold watch," I repeated to myself, thrilled by the pleasure of the internal slant rhymes linking *set* and *fat* with *watch*, binding *love* to *gold*. As if suddenly hearing them for the first time, I loved, too, the succinct Plathian stresses and monosyllables *(love-set-you, fat-gold-watch)* as they fired off the opening line that propelled the poem forward. What I loved most about "Morning Song," however, was its vulnerability. Unlike the work that had been assigned to me as an undergraduate—poems in which a vengeful speaker plays the part of scorned daughter or lover—"Morning Song" displays real humility. As she attends her infant, the mother-speaker is exhausted, stupefied, clumsy, smitten, weighted by obligation. And yet, in spite of itself (and unlike a great deal of Plath's work), "Morning Song" ends on a note of brightness and levity: the "clear vowels" of the baby's cry rising "like balloons" as dawn's first light floods the household.

There's no adequate way to explain the extent to which having a child revises the illusion of self. For poets who also mother, the working life is likewise altered as one fights for scraps of time, or struggles to navigate how best to write (or not write) about one's offspring. Although Eavan Boland's characterization of Plath's hardships those final autumn and winter months was moving, particularly in terms of caring for Nicolas and Frieda, what ultimately changed my mind about Plath wasn't the fact of her motherhood; rather, it was how motherhood reshaped her on the page. Returning to *The Collected Poems* after hearing Boland's explication of "Balloons," I began to notice a powerful evolution in the writing over time. As she drafts in the last season of her life—poems about roasting Sunday lamb, passing before mirrors, letter-writing, bee-keeping, pushing the pram, night feeding, tidying up holiday decor—Plath's gaze seems less fixated on an internalized mythologized self and, instead, turned outward toward the ordinary. What results is a rich hybridity, a blending of competing impulses pre- and post-parenthood. While Plath's voice-driven stanzas still rush headlong down the page, in other words, they do so with a different consciousness.

Consider, for instance, "Nick and the Candlestick," which reflects Plath's inclination toward theatricality and artifice, as well as her rendering of domestic reality. It's interesting to note that Plath produces "Nick and the Candlestick" on the same day that she completes "Lady Lazarus"—perhaps the strongest example of the poet's self-mythologizing. "Nick and the Candlestick" is different, however. For seven stanzas, Plath does what many feel she does best; that is, she manifests an eerie world of extended metaphor. Guided by Plath's speaker, who has transformed herself into a "miner," readers enter the cave of a nursery ornamented with homicides, black bats, icy panes, piranhas. This invented world is hyperbolic, fragmented, and narrated via a childlike sonic repetition. It is also unapologetically dramatic and self-referential. In line twenty-three, however, Plath abandons the descriptive and declarative modes to directly address the infant: "O love," she asks, "how did you get here?" Unlike in the poem's upper half, the diction here is simple and stripped of the figurative. From this point, Plath writes with even greater clarity, using longer sentences to characterize her feeling for the child. It isn't the laboring miner's voice we hear, however—another example of Plath's long-relied-upon personas—but the unmasked mother who affectionately casts Nick as "the one / solid the spaces lean on."

In her essay, "Mommy Poems; or, Writing as the Muse Herself," Rachel Richardson argues that, in her poems of parenthood, Plath performs a disappearing act, a kind of self-erasure that's often demanded of women but one that is being enthusiastically resisted by contemporary writers who depict mothers as more than spectators or mere receptacles (a point with which I agree). I might add, however, that in the case of Plath's speakers, this receding of self—or at the very least, the stripping down of persona—actually serves the larger body of work. It's when Plath steps away from the center and moves toward the margins of the room that we see and hear a more complex version of the poet. Perhaps this is because unlike the other players who populate Plath's work—fathers, aunts, lovers, biblical figures, doctors, jailers, gods—Nicolas and Frieda provide a counter-presence that isn't adversarial. To state things even more simply: I believe that, after years of self-dramatization and relying on persona as a primary shaping device, as a poet, Plath needed to get out of her own way. One means of accomplishing this was to further invite the domestic into the work by writing directly from the more intimate perspective of mother.

The years we lived in England, I was unwell. In the arc from summer to spring, I fought what felt like an endless string of fevers, sinus infections, sore throats, flu, depression. Blood panels produced no leads. One physician suggested that I had "expat syndrome"—meaning, my immune system was ill-equipped to deal with Oxford's dampness. Another doctor suspected I was allergic to mold. My husband often traveled for weeks at a time, leaving me alone with our young children. Thousands of miles from friends and family, I was lonely, sleep-deprived, exhausted. Playing the part of trailing spouse, the dutiful foreign service officer's wife, I learned to walk in rain without complaint, pushing our three-year-old in her covered stroller to the grocery store and music class without an umbrella. As months went by, the sense of isolation worsened, but the weather bothered me less. Only now, looking back, do I realize how elements of my life overlapped with Plath's: our shared experiences as foreigners married to professionally lauded spouses; the toll of always serving as the supporting player; the difficulty of mothering while fighting mental illness; the struggle of interrogating the darkness while the children slept.

I'm drafting this essay in a hotel room purchased via an app that offers cheap last-minute deals—a Valentine's gift from my husband, who's at home watching the kids. This three-night stay is the first protected writing time I've had in more than four years. With quiet comes opportunity for reflection. I've been thinking about our last year in England, how one night we went to sleep in London's autumn and woke to winter: the sky, a crisp misplaced blue that stings the skin and hurts one's ears. Although I didn't make the connection at the time, my journals reveal that it was Plath's birthday. Before returning to Oxford, I asked to visit the house on Fitzroy where Yeats once lived and Plath later died. Too embarrassed to play literary tourist by snapping photos of the neighborhood, I used the stop in Primrose Hill as an excuse to walk our dog, passing the pale green house with its blue historical plaque, white trim, sandy brickwork. 23 Fitzroy's door is glossy black—so black it shines—in the right light, you might even catch your reflection in it. Before seeing the building in person, I didn't realize its flats extend down as well as up. At an iron guardrail, I peered beneath the street-level into a basement kitchen whose remodeled granite countertops surprised me. While the dog peed, I took note of the flat's steel refrigerator, what must have been an oven's face, a bottle of household cleaner, abandoned dishrag. No sign of any tenants. The whole thing took less than two minutes.

We then rounded the corner to 3 Chalcot Square to see the other flat, the one Plath shared with Ted Hughes before the couple abandoned London for Court Green in Devon. The house, now pink, is grander than its Fitzroy counterpart with front pillars and large windows overlooking the gardens. Its oval marker reads, "Sylvia Plath . . . lived here 1960–1961" (no mention of the husband). There were other dog-walkers that morning, a city worker collecting bins of leaves and garden rubbish, a woman who pushed a bassinette while shushing an infant. I stood near the house and tried not to stare, imagining Plath making sandwiches or readying Frieda before taking her to see the lions at nearby Regent's Zoo. I even remembered how, from the open windows of their sitting room, Plath and Hughes reported hearing seals barking. For a while, our children played tag in the adjacent park, a small green and tree-lined space that boasts some minor play equipment. Out of breath, they returned for a snack. Beside us on the bench, a stranger tore off two small pieces of sourdough from the loaf he was holding, offered them to my son and daughter. What, I wonder, is the risk of disclosure in the country of motherhood? What is the risk of suspending and restaging any moment in time? Somewhere, in a kitchen in England, an American mother is painting a leafy pattern on her toddler's chair. Her phone rings. The kettle sings. A poem might be made of it.

Savage Flower: One Mother Writing War

PAMELA HART

> Only make you a mother, which is the last savage flower
> —Rachel Zucker, "What Dark Thing"

Here's a war story. It takes place one night in a parking lot after my support group meeting on post-traumatic stress disorder and how to recognize it in your soldier. One mother is going on about her son. How he came home changed because he saw his sergeant killed. And that I need to remember to send extra socks to my son when he's over there. Meantime, I'm counting the Red Cross rescue vehicles, noticing the way streetlights pool their beams on the pavement. This, I'm thinking then, won't happen to my son.

When my son enlisted in the Army, I went looking for war stories. I was hungry for fiction and nonfiction, poetry, film, even television. I especially wanted stories that represented those at home—the family members of the women and men who have served and deployed, some more than once, for nearly two decades.

This desire begins as a yearning for connection. At support group meetings, most of us are women: mothers, spouses, fiancées, and, as the months go by, a baby or two. We describe worries and fears, share emails from our soldier, discuss whether to tune into the news or not. The conversations become a way for me to think not only about myself but about poetry. I understand that war is written through women's—mothers'—bodies. That I might fill a gap by giving voice and shape to home-front narratives.

In this way, war, mothering, and writing engender a complicated space of creation. Even as they collide—how much to reveal in a poem about one's child/self—my writing at the outskirts of war becomes a necessary process of making sense. I also understand that without poems and prose by women, particularly mothers, depictions of what poet Muriel Rukeyser has called the "concept of perpetual warfare" privilege the soldier's view, obscuring war's impact beyond the battlefield. The landscape of this long war, of most wars, focuses primarily on the warrior.

And then how to write into experiences that are not my own? Because the stories are accumulating. Even as I obtain permission from family members to interview them, explaining I'm not writing news but making poetry, their words sit anxiously in my notebook. I cross exam my perspective and presence as I listen, take notes, and write.

For instance, the word *complicit*, with its various etymological strands connected to weave and fold, appears in one of my early notebooks. I'm definitely tangled up in questions circling violence, war, self, the son, and poetry. Because to imagine, a visionary act nested within creativity, is becoming a kind of participation. So picture a room without doors or windows filling with water. How to escape before you drown—stop imagining.

Instead I write a poem about improvised explosive devices. A young soldier who has completed Ranger School with my son steps on an IED while on patrol in Afghanistan. I follow his survival and progress on social media. The conventions of a poem seem absurd. I can't bear line breaks. Syntax seems artificial. Punctuation feels wrong. I'm not a war poet and can't manage meter. Eventually the poetry of Kimiko Hahn leads me to the *zuihitsu*, meaning "a running brush." Its fragmented, associative, collage-like prose form suits my mind. The process of writing in this way cracks something open. I understand the home front, while not a combat zone, is as beautiful and dangerous.

Writing the book goes on for years, as does the war. My research includes interviews, time at various military posts, plus binging on television and film, as well as reading widely within the war literature canon, which, like most canons, overlooks certain narratives. I begin to mentor women writers in Afghanistan, some of whom travel from remote areas and risk their safety to write about lives, impacted by war and oppression. Always there's the news. Freelance journalist James Foley is kidnapped in Syria by the Islamic State. I read the diary of Guantanamo Bay prisoner Mohammedou Ould Slahi. It's wrong to watch the Foley video posted online. I confess this in the poem I write even as I continue to look. My son deploys. Foley is murdered. Slahi's book becomes a best seller. Barbara Guest writes that a poem's "hidden anxiety" urges a deeper searching. "A poem should tremble a little," she says in her book *Forces of Imagination*. I check the Faces of the Fallen website. And continue to work on a shivery poem that references jumpsuits, orange, James Foley, and looking.

Once upon a time, a soldier friend of my son's, about to leave for Afghanistan, takes me for a ride in the sports car he has just purchased. Soon after I discern a frightening impulse to become everyone's mother, which is arrogant, impossible, and perhaps part of the American story of empire. Is it witness, documentation, or hubris? I determine to look closely at this inclination as I write.

In *The Things They Carried*, Tim O'Brien's now classic book of stories on the Vietnam war, he says, "A true war story . . . is never about war. It's about love and memory. It's about sorrow." Still, home-front literature is marginalized. It's too domestic/romanticized/sentimental. Also the country is disconnected, disinterested. How I disdain the president's dismissal of one family's loss when he remarks to the widow of a soldier killed in combat, "He knew what he signed up for." Since 9/11 nearly three million service members have served on 5.4 million deployments. They have parents, siblings, spouses, children, yet the home front of this long war doesn't really exist in popular culture and art. As Ilya Kaminsky writes in his latest collection, *Deaf Republic*, "we (forgive us) lived happily during the war."

And yet. Rukeyser says in her book *The Life of Poetry* that the history of this country is built on the idea of war, "but around and under and above it is another reality . . . the history of possibility."

Here's another story. In the time before my son heads down range I spend an hour looking at a stream as it charges endlessly over the tops of boulders. The forces of water and flow make crystalline waves that explode across the rocks. For a while I forget everything and nothing is true—only the water, the rock, and the flow.

from "On Writing 'Cajas/Boxes with Zero Tolerance'"

EMMY PÉREZ

On writing a "crown" of undone "sonnets" in Summer 2018:

Summer 2018, my daughter A. was six years old. My son J. was four.

When I told them what was going on with asylum-seeking families, because I usually tell them what's going on, J. immediately asked, "Is that going to happen to us?"

They'd already attended No Border Wall, César Chávez Day, Climate Day marches, and the like, so they were aware, I assumed, that we had the privilege to protest.

But J. was somewhat panicked and it surprised me. He likely learned panic from me. I was pissed, deeply hurt, and mourning for the families, and yes, panicking for the families, for human rights. I expressed most on paper, but I did not pretend around my kids that all was cheery as Peppa Pig here in the Tejas borderlands.

I paused in responding, however, somewhat relieved that children his age may still believe that all experience the same protections. I likely hadn't explained why people seek asylum.

I wanted to alleviate his worry, but as I thought of *how* to explain it, I let him sit in discomfort for a bit. Could this be the start of a greater empathy? The delicate balance between the binary of "this could be us next" or "no, this could never happen to us," so you're off the hook.

Must we encourage children to try walking in other people's shoes? I do this, but do we *need* to as a first resort? He did so automatically. How to encourage "let me love people I don't know, let me recognize their suffering and act for social justice"?

I wanted to avoid guilt-inducing parenting shortcuts as someone who was often parented that way. That method usually shuts down all conversation completely.

Here was the identity and privilege talk J. and I needed to have (his sister was further along), though it was hard to find the right words because the quickest answers would imply that some children are *better than* others, wouldn't they? Yuck. I recall thinking how awful the easy answers would sound: "Because you were born here, because I was born here and your grandparents were born here, and the migrants were not." "You're U.S. American, Tejanx, Mexican American, Xicanx." "*They* were born in other countries and now seek asylum here." "45 and his cronies create horrifying policies like walls and separating families because they make their unfair voters happy."

Too many come to distinguish themselves from immigrants as a point of pride, forgetting they may have first said "but I was born here" as a defense against racial profiling and xenophobia. Rarely are we conditioned to say, "I was born here, but in the founding of this country, the original peoples of this land have been displaced and worse," unless our peoples are indeed from here since for always. I grew up in Southern California wounded by the word "wetback" and white people who assumed I didn't speak English based on the color of my brown skin. How many downright dangerous comebacks did we create in our minds, ready to launch the next time: *Ha, ha, you call me wetback? You shout, "Go back to Mexico!" Well, I was born here.*

My children know I'm proud that we have native roots in México, las américas, Turtle Island.

Meanwhile, institutionalized white patriarchal supremacy wants us to assimilate (obey), though always remain a class lower, and if you are also a woman, gender non-binary, or a member of another oppressed group, then another notch(es) lower. Discrimination has no foreseeable end.

I've built this up to share what I eventually told J., but I draw a blank. Perhaps I failed. I can tell you that my children and I then protested family separation with the community outside of "La Hielera" with the infamous cages and other locations in McAllen. I don't take them to all the protests that I attend in the Rio Grande Valley, but they've gone to many. On June 17, 2018, Father's Day, they stood for a long time in very hot weather, hair drenched, taking turns sitting in the stroller, at other times holding their signs with pride, other times complaining of the heat, and other times chanting with others.

One time a year later, only J. and I went to a protest outside of the Ursula Detention Center. We made our posters at home. With green marker, he drew a rectangle with three small cages inside of it, with three faces inside each one, one with a sad face and the others just circles with no eyes or mouths. He drew an X that covered the entire rectangle and drew another X beside the rectangle. Underneath it, he drew another child smiling outdoors, grass beneath, and placed a check mark next to the child. I loved his clear message of right and wrong, though I hoped he wasn't only imagining himself out and other less fortunate children in and suffering—but good start.

I recall poems I wrote in 2014, the year J. was born, about unaccompanied youth crossing the borderlands as they were in the tens of thousands. In one of them that I rarely ever share at readings anymore because I have since questioned its approach, I imagine out loud what it would be like as a mother saying good-bye to their young children leaving to seek asylum. It's not a dramatic monologue, but a poem in which the narrator states the reality of her privilege and then imagines.

About a year later, I began writing poems about children and families crossing the Mediterranean Sea after I saw the photo of three-year-old Alan Kurdi on the beach. And in 2017, the photo of five-year-old Omran Daqneesh sitting shell-shocked in an ambulance immediately reminded me of J., who was three at the time. I can't recall if I wrote about that photo or if I felt terrible for days thinking about the horrors of war, and yes, how it would affect me as a mother. I think it's dangerous to say that only parents can imagine what it must be like to lose a child in war, and that is not what I mean to suggest here.

I usually write something in response to events immediately, but I didn't write much in response to the photo of Óscar and Valeria Ramírez. Local activists I admire were urging folx to remove the photo of father and daughter face down in the nearby river from their social media and urging them to instead post photos of them while alive. I'd heard something similar in 2015 about the ethics of writing about the little boy washed up on the beach.

I have all but abandoned the poems that caused me to question the ethics of writing them shortly after doing so. Maybe I needed to write them, but feel I haven't gotten them quite right yet.

Demetria Martinez recently shared an interview in the *Brooklyn Rail* with Martín Espada, in which he states that "the alternative is silence" if we poets avoid writing this work.

Why can't I finish this essay, and why can't I finish the poem sequence?

Part of why is because my own poems wound me. Part of why is because I don't want them to wound others. Part of why is because the truth is a wound. Part of why is because I don't want to think about it anymore. Part of why is because disassociation is how I have survived other kinds of trauma in my life. And what does it even mean to survive trauma? To be alive? Part of why is because I cannot do enough to help on the ground with a full-time job, children, and more. It could become all-consuming. Even cooking at home is a miracle and I haven't slept enough since before my children were born in order to get everything done. Part of why is because six or so months before I started writing the poem sequence, a man ran a red light and T-boned my vehicle, which left me with concussion, neck, back injuries no amount of time "off" of work could heal. Thankfully, my son's car seat worked better than my seatbelt. It took me six months to get behind the wheel again. Part of why is because of susto.

Part of why is because the creeping Gen-X pull-yourself-up-by-the bootstraps notion of "aren't all of these just excuses" for not doing more direct service/action, despite the fact that some of the most dedicated, non-paid activists who help migrants don't have small children, or that they have flexible schedules with unrelated employment. Thank goodness as well for retired individuals who can financially afford to use their time for greater good. Writers with children can stay up after their children have gone to bed, though exhaustion is real.

This is anecdotal, but there are also many volunteers that come from outside of the community during their alternative spring breaks and summer vacations and such, which is a good thing while also reinforcing the privilege many have to do this work. A few weeks in the summer, with paid childcare, I volunteered with a center's off-site storage unit, unpacking and organizing donations. On other days inside of the center, I helped make sandwiches, sanitized napping areas, but could never stay late enough to help serve when hundreds arrived after ICE dropped them off after being released from La Hielera, the adults with ankle monitors. I made childcare arrangements so that I could help a few late afternoons/early evenings as well, but I was almost turned away because the volunteer coordinator said something like "since you live here, you can come back anytime when we need more volunteers, and right now we have people visiting from out of town."

"I'm sorry, I can't come back anytime," I replied, briefly explaining my full-time teaching job and motherhood. It had taken me four years to make it into the center. There I stood, finally. In 2014, I yearned to help, but had just given birth to J., and his sister was only two.

That late afternoon / early evening, I helped exhausted parents bathe their children while teenagers from out of town sat in bunches, combing children's hair. We had plenty to keep us busy.

That summer 2018, I also helped Angry Tias and Abuelas RGV, thanks to co-founder Nayelly Barrios, who years before was one of my poetry students. We bought and carried supplies to asylum seekers on the bridge in Reynosa, where metering was taking place, and another time, I helped another Tia assist asylum seekers at the McAllen bus station. Just a tiny amount of volunteer work, but it helped me better understand.

In one of the poems, I wrote of feeling helpless to truly help, how I never wanted to be a lawyer or be independently wealthy until now, to help reunify and help pay for reunification flights. And in another poem I'm still writing, I'm responding to Steve Bannon's "Just give me more. Tear down more statues. Say the revolution is coming. I can't get enough of it"—said after people reacted to the horror of Charlottesville by toppling confederate statues and the like. What feels like taunting and reverse psychology he claimed was rooted in 45's ratings going up.

I always return to the failure of poetry to do enough. The work is not only about our pain, but we cannot deny the pain that prompts us to write the work in the first place. What is the nature of empathy—what do we do with it when we can't do much else? What can we realistically commit to, to help?

My literary commitment is to finish this work.

Poster children Stephen Miller, 45, Jeff Sessions, Kirstjen Nielsen, et al. did little to help reunify beyond "discontinuing" the policy. Their new policies are traumatizing as well. Family separation continued—and continues—beyond spring and summer 2018, and in fact, the testing ground of separations began in El Paso in 2017. The authoritarians weren't scrambling to keep track, nor were they scrambling to reunify—they needed a lawsuit and subsequent judge's orders with deadlines to force them to reunify and they continued to fail. A ton of volunteers helped with the initial reunifications, and they were not volunteering on behalf of the administration, they were volunteering against the administration, in spite of the administration. They were doing, with love, what the administration would not do.

We don't have to disassociate to experience joy living near the militarized river. I write because I want to explore the extremes and depths. It's not always easy for me, however.

The second time I gave birth, I decided not to have an epidural like the first time. I wanted to feel what women experience and have experienced for millennia. I admit that I may have felt some of my trauma surfacing that evening, disassociated, and delaying the birth by a few hours. The power of the mind.

Maybe too these poems help me feel and remember the range of my humanity before the inevitable disassociation.

I must want others to feel more too. Reading articles, seeing reunification photos and videos helps. But what happens next?

❧

Do I know how to write a healing poem to myself? Do I know how to heal from childhood silences and trauma?

You always convince yourself you should be pouring love into thinking of others besides yourself. Because you have food. Because you have shelter. Because you have citizenship, health insurance, retirement funds someday.

Instructions: Write a love letter to yourself.

❧

What else do I need to do to finish this crown? First, they are not a crown. They are an uncrowning. Uncrown the kings and queens in the poems. I'm gonna uncrown them and not crown anyone else.

❧

Today, March 19, 2020, amid COVID-19 worries, I asked J., now six, what he remembers of that time almost two years ago. The first thing he says is "Why do they say 'break bread?'" I'm surprised he remembers the #BreakBreadNotFamilies action. I explained it means we should all sit down and eat together as family instead of separating families. The twenty-four-day fast chain ended with participants breaking bread together.

I asked if he knows why people seek asylum. He thought it was only for economic reasons. Just a few days ago, he read Duncan Tonatiuh's *Undocumented: A Worker's Fight*. For this quarantine time, I'd laid out some books that had been previously buried in piles, and he chose it. I explained why people seek asylum, what happens with family separation, and asked if he remembers asking me if we'd be separated too. He said no, but asked again if they could separate us. Back to square one, but not really.

"What do you think we should do to help?" I asked.

"Try to change the border's mind," he said, "or try to get another president."

I asked A., now eight, "Do you remember the chant *Gobierno mentirosa, el pueblo está furioso?*"

"Yes," she said.

"You liked chanting that, didn't you?"

"Yeah."

"Why?"

"Because he's a liar."

On Mothering and Reading

CHANDA FELDMAN

It was 2014. I worked overlapping short-term jobs: teaching creative writing online, private English language tutoring, and freelance writing. My almost three-year-old son was in day care and my six-month-old daughter was home with me. My husband was a postdoctoral student.

Our daily routine was predictable and simultaneously perpetually new: cooking, ferrying kids, naps, breastfeeding, diaper changes, house cleaning, play dates, work schedules, a new baby tooth breaking through, syllables conglomerating into a first word, an important work deadline, a high fever and rash, a holiday celebration.

Amidst these rhythms, I wasn't writing very much. New poems were few and too far apart. My poetry manuscript was too short and seemed far from that rumored, heavenly circumstance of "and then everything just fell into place." I worried I had exhausted my poetic themes and ideas and I worried because I was often too exhausted to write.

This is a brief narrative, paved, for the ease of telling. I don't want to diminish or quickly alleviate the frustration and fear I felt over not writing, but I want to tell you a little about how I started writing again and what I wrote about. I located a way forward in my reading life. The two texts that helped me come to motherhood as a generative subject were a video of Junot Díaz interviewing Toni Morrison at the New York Public Library in December 2013, and the poet Eavan Boland's nonfiction book, *A Journey with Two Maps*.

Everything Toni Morrison said in her interview with Junot Díaz was memorable. At forty-two minutes in, Morrison recounts the story of Margaret Garner's escape from slavery, subsequent capture, and her murdering her two-year-old-daughter rather than returning her child to slavery as the inspiration for her novel *Beloved*. The abolitionists wanted Garner put to death for her crime, but the slave owners wanted her charged, ". . . guilty of theft, the theft of herself and theft of her children." Around the forty-four-minute mark, Morrison transitions to the feminist currents in the air in 1983, when *Beloved* was published: there was talk of "breaking glass ceilings" and centering a woman's freedom on the choice to have children and abortion access. Morrison says, "And I was thinking just the opposite . . . I never felt more free in my life until I had children. It was just the opposite of a burden . . . and I thought for Black women enslaved to have a child that you were responsible for, that was really yours, that was really freedom . . . you didn't have children, you may have produced them but they weren't yours." Slavery broke up Black families and my own family history reflects this fact, but I hadn't quite viewed becoming a mother as an act of freedom, as a privilege of choice. I heard Toni Morrison radicalizing mothering, and Black mothering in particular, as a source of power and free will to create a present and future.

Morrison's words needled a memory for me as well, or the inheritance of a memory from my mother. This memory appears in a fourteen-poem sequence called, "But We Lived," from my book, *Approaching the Fields*, that I would begin writing in the days after watching the interview.

A recognition of motherhood in the history that catalyzed Morrison felt as if it reached through my mother to me. In the poem, "But We Lived. 2. Sharecropping," segregation is a fact, but the devastation lodges in Mrs. Hughes' exercise, as a White woman, as the parents' employer and debtor, to act with unquestioned authority to separate parent and child.

My family sharecropped at the Hughes' place.

The Hughes' owned the Movie Palace in town,
our little house. They had a pond our church
baptized in. I remember Mrs. Hughes

scolded my parents: it's too cold in the fields
for that child.

The mother in this poem is robbed of her agency to care for, protect, or exercise preference over her own child's whereabouts. I wrote poems about race, economics, class, and the Jim Crow era, but I had not considered deeply this history from the position of mothering or being mothered under these conditions. I had not explored in writing how one mothers and attempts, in the ways available to them, to keep a child safe and whole in a racialized world that is hostile to them, in a racialized world that will, with certainty, threaten them psychically and very likely physically. The space of a poem began to open up for me from the subject position of being a Black mother.

Around the time I saw the Morrison interview, I was also reading poet Eavan Boland's nonfiction book, *A Journey with Two Maps: Becoming a Woman Poet*. She describes early motherhood with toys and plastic cups about her new suburban Dublin home, her writing notebook mixed among these things. What called to me was her description of a struggle to shape a poem that made use of the objects and dailiness of her life as a mother. The book manifested to me the crucial inclusion of the domestic sphere in the poem, insisting on literal domestic interiors as settings being inhabited in the ways they are actually inhabited.

Landscape, flora and fauna, and the external world foregrounded many of my poems. I was taking my poems indoors. I was looking for mothers and children in the home like homes I knew. I remembered Natasha Trethewey's *Domestic Work*, a book of poems dear to me, with many poems locating mother and daughter amidst a home life's intimacies and tensions. How and why had I stayed outside for so long in my poems? In "Interior," I took a poem into a house:

> My grandmother walked the field road
>
> home to birth my mother in her room.
> My mother slept there as a child in a bed
>
> at her parents' feet. The floor's worn
> wide-plank boards. The bureau's oblong
>
> and oval mirror missing a piece. My mother
> signed her mother's name to the letter.

For me, this poem isn't interested in joy or sorrow: its alliance is with home life as a humanizing space with its own history, its private arrangements of family, its motherhood and daughterhood interacting as dynamic, radical forces of ordinary being and care.

I would say Morrison and Boland's words re-orientated me, guiding me when I was in need of a new course in my writing and personal life to integrate my new knowledge of motherhood.

Writing Prompts

Prompts in this part ask you to consider the world around you. How might imagery, stories, and sounds from the world around you seep into your poems? How might the world mark you or your child and cast your parenting in a new light? These prompts ask that as you and your child move through the world, you attune yourself to the ways the world intrudes or sparks delight.

1) In "My Daughter Returns from My Ex-Wife's House with Braids in Her Hair," the braid, referred to as "another woman's twists," becomes a symbol of the daughter's life, separate from the speaker, out in the world. In this poem, the speaker wants to "undo" this symbol as a way to reclaim her daughter.

   When your child returns from "the world"—whether that is a trip to the playground, to school, to work, or somewhere further afield—what marks of the world do they bring with them? Make a list of those marks or objects, and then pick one to be the central symbol in your poem.

   Consider your feelings about where your child has been. Like Allison Blevins, let your description of that symbol show the reader how you feel about your child's trip into the world.

2) Sara Mumolo takes something that is often not considered "poetic"—the need to earn money—and makes it the basis for her poem "10 weeks and intermittent: earning." Camille T. Dungy's poem describes the challenges of traveling with a small child. What is something that is part of your everyday life with your child that feels completely un-poetic? Incorporate it in a poem.

Mumolo's piece, like Tina Chang's and Pamela Hart's, is a prose poem—written as a block of text instead of incorporating line breaks. Using this or another prompt in the book, shape your piece into a prose poem and see how the lack of line breaks affects the movement of words and ideas. You might, like Chang, write in full sentences, or, like Mumolo and Hart, choose fragments. Could you use repetition or syllables with strong stresses to create even more rhythm?

3) In "Suicide Prevention" the speaker sees a sign that she does not want to explain to her child. What are the things you have wanted to avoid discussing with a child? Write a poem that explores your avoidance of one of the topics on your list.

4) In "Homeland Security," "Cajas/Boxes with Zero Tolerance #9," and "Monster," poets position their thoughts about parenting against current and historical events. Pick an event from the news or history that evokes strong feelings about being a parent.
   a) Like Nicole Cooley, allude to that event in your poem about parenting.
   b) Like Emmy Pérez, pick a quote from the news and use the words you find there to become the backbone of your poem.
   c) Like Natalie Shapero, name the event and juxtapose it against your images of parenting.

5) Clarissa Mendiola's "Nearly There" contains Mendiola's son's beautiful observation about his family's appearance and their native landscape: "Mommy, we are brown because / we come from an island." Children make startling observations about the world. Keep a list of things your child observes about the world and use one as the opening of a poem.

Transitions

IN PARENTING THE ONLY CONSTANT IS CHANGE. THE 2020 documentary *Babies* reminds us that in their first year, bodies grow more than they ever will again. Phases like "the terrible twos" and teething and night terrors feel survivable because we trust that they are just phases, that they, too, will pass. Between birth and eighteen years, we mark several distinct stages in life—infancy, childhood, tweens, and teens—and yet seasoned parents everywhere assure new parents that the time will pass in an instant. This part considers not only the remarkable transitions children undergo but also ways that parents transition in response to children. Several of these poems use unconventional forms to examine possible futures or links to the past, suggesting that the poem itself can create a kind of transitional space in which new possibilities arise.

Some writers in this part are at early stages of transition. Faylita Hicks writes of the journey toward giving up a child for adoption, and Sunu P. Chandy of adopting a child transnationally, acclimating that child to a new culture and world. Others are in later stages—Lena Khalaf Tuffaha, Mahogany L. Browne, and Angela Narciso Torres consider how their relationship with their children changes as those children grow through the teen years.

Other mothers undergo their own transformations. Both Melissa Stephenson and Emari DiGiorgio measure personal transitions in relationship with nature. Stephenson watches the cycles of robins and falcons, measuring them against her movement through her child's illness and her own struggles. DiGiorgio transitions into a world of mothers that transcends species; in "Fallible Beasts," she comes to identify with the gorilla Harambe's mother, Kayla. Sasha West considers the changing planet in both her poem "Recognition" and her essay "War Songs: Mothering through Climate Change." In a section of her long poem "Whereas," Layli Long Soldier contemplates the way her relationship to being Lakota must evolve so that she can share her culture with her daughter. Teri Ellen Cross Davis has transitioned into "the tension of motherhood / and career, poet and wife." Her attempt to manage multiple identities brings Plath to mind, and she weaves her story together with Plath's. Some transformations are both physical and metaphysical: Jordan Rice's essay contemplates gender transition alongside the transition into parenthood; and Kim-An Lieberman, whose "More Moon" was published in a posthumous collection, juxtaposes her own imminent death from gastric cancer with her child's awakening to language and nature.

There are several experimental poems in this part. Brenda Shaughnessy and Sun Yung Shin write poems about speculative futures; Shaughnessy's imagines "Our Family on the Run" during an apocalypse; Shin's pushes families further and further into a future in which parents become irrelevant and children become marionettes. Sarah Vap's poem uses the process of mothering to transform her writing, incorporating her child's found speech into the poem as the child speaks. Just as the mother's life is a series of constant interruptions, the poem is in a state of constant interruption, breaking from its meditation on kings, brides, and bridegrooms into "Put ladder // on fire truck?" Finally, Vanessa Angélica Villarreal reminds us that our human minds can not even comprehend the way time works and generations transition in her merger of poetry and computer code in "ƒ = [*(root) (future)*]." She exhorts the child to "learn from this. . . / Time was never a line, but a field & you are occurring / alongside the past."

Two of the essays in this part are also process oriented, delineating ways that both Emari DiGiorgio and Melissa Stephenson developed new writing routines in the most hectic early days of mothering. For parents and non-parents alike, their paths are instructive. Perhaps more important, they provide hope that no matter what our current life circumstances, we can maintain a connection to our writing.

The Whole Point

LENA KHALAF TUFFAHA

My first time like a fool I insisted—no epidural for me.
I shook so violently I thought I would die right then,
no poems published yet, so much left unsaid.
Turns out we are stronger and
more stubborn than we imagine.

I told the story many times.
Girlfriends and aunties love testimony from the frontlines.
But you are almost thirteen now,
and the memories recede.

When I first glimpsed you, dark eyes wide open,
I knew something between us had ended.
The quiet companionship,
the cocoon we both lived in cast aside.

Later, with your sisters,
you prepared me for this loss.
I knew to lean in to the quiet and listen,
to learn their language before they could speak it,
before the exit from wordless music
into out-loud song.

A million farewells follow this day.
The guilt-heavy wanting to leave you for the first time,
craving back some of the space you have taken,
trying to assemble the puzzle of self after you.
Sharing your heart with friends, your adoration with teachers.

At school the principal tells us:
We really value independence.
We want to teach them how to leave the nest, the whole point is
to prepare them to go out into the world.

We have been. From the moment you arrived in our arms,
giving you pieces of ourselves, amulets from our journey,
and kissing you good-bye.

The Birth Mother's Red Bath for Courage

FAYLITA HICKS

With spoiled milk seeping
from its many small brown mouths,
my body twitched loose the dead
skin snaked around it, dripped
runes in the doorway,
heaved bullet after bullet
into the tub—but did not die.
There are claw marks
& hot grease stains
where things came through.
Signature survival signs
etched around my belly—
at the hinge, in the crevices.
All of it evidence: I did give birth
to something. There was a killing here—
of a kind. Something is lost now,
forced from a room in me. Something
is stifled in this body; I have become
a deconstructed basket
of rose-colored towels
singing on the hospital's floor.
Some nights, I think this body
must still be calling out to the child
that tore through it or trying to
forgive itself for giving itself over
to the strange & inconvenient truth
that not all mothers—are mothers.
Some mothers are war—an enemy
of their own desires. Some mothers
are graveyards—a field of want
buried beneath other fields of want.
Some nights, I think this body
must still be praying to a god
that has long since slithered away.

from *Winter: Aphorisms*

SARAH VAP

Someone cries every few minutes in our family
for the past four and a half years. My older son is crying because he has to go upstairs
to get dressed. My younger son is crying because he can't go upstairs.

King Lear, I tell them,

said Never never never never never. King Lear, I tell them, like all of you

said No no no. King Lear, they say back, their fingers curled

by their noses like sneaky rats, their noses curled
and both of the little boys

walking like creeps on their tiptoes, *as if we are each*

(I see them signal) *God's loosening spies—*

❧

Dada, come ah-on! Says the baby waggling all his fat fingers at Dada. Dada, come on, says his older
brother more clearly. I am the pattern of all patience! he replies. Jesus,

not Lear,

I remind him, first revealed himself a king

at a wedding.

Revealed himself at the wedding, my husband replies,
between the fat and bones

of the king who is locked

inside too many skins.

Between the wine wearing thin
at midnight and the miracle wine—, I declare, became king

of the bride and the bridegroom, king
of that bed. Put ladder

on fire truck? Yes, sweetheart, I continue: he slipped

to the bed of their bodies, slipped to the bed

of their ordinary marriage and between even
those lovers making love, I tell my son, he was king.

They were three kings, their mouths touching,

my husband raptures, *the lover-kings*—.

That marriage,

he throws the fire truck to the floor, pissed, not for lovers!
That the marriage for the *pirate* to the *soldier*,

my son continues, *and it cuts off their heads.*

Where a person might pause—
to *stop*,
that is the mercy. Child. With no stop
there is no mercy: and our own

lives in it. Women
reveal themselves in children.
Men
reveal themselves in deeds and acts

or even the coherence

of his mind. The coherence

of the mind of the child. Cohering
of the man and the woman or thus

the coherence of the child: to flatten,

to encroach, or to retreat.

Night carries the stars as it turns. As water

is moved slowly by cupped hands—

the family moves through each night: the family is a clear
sphere. Inside all the other clear spheres

and holding within itself

all the clear spheres and all of them turning
clocks. Mama, I have to go potty. Okay sweetheart. And all the moments

of every clock are the unfolding

or the loosening mind. Correct and test

the folds and unfolds

against your life. Mama, I'll yell
when you have to wipe my butt. Against a broader commonwealth:

of moans, slipping. Slipping through the humans.

Slipping through the animals.

Slipping to the rock—moans.
Moans

that you may
or you may not know.

❧

Mama, poop is coming out of my butt.

Okay, honey.

Does that make you real happy?

Yes.

❧

Slipping, we will lose winter, altogether. Our home, just a few feet
from the melt-off of one of the world's last glaciers: there will be the moment

when it actually stops.

To freeze, I tell my son, is not the same
as to stop.

❧

Slipping, we will lose winter, altogether. The whole
of the mountain will lose winter.

The mind will lose winter as our world becomes—. Night is the mind

that cools in the earth's shadow.

❧

We're held inside that shadow

for exactly the time needed
to distill a particular star out

of the greater light of the sun—we're held within night

exactly the lengths and cuts of time needed to dim

that mind of the sun.

❧

That's a pirate fallen into the water.

And that's a terrible pirate crawling over a log.

That's a volcano and that is a hole of fire.

The sun?

Yes, the hole of fire.

Tonight the snow

floated upward into
incessant rain while the neighbor's lost peacock wept

and our cup runneth—it's true, what they say: the cock

calls out to you and me like a baby sobbing.

❧

And after the long rain.

And after that

a break in the falling—and the long
gray month. And another. And the daytime

barely distinguishes itself from the night. Then maybe
silence as all the parts

move smoothly across and together and apart
from one another. Remember: thrumming,

mingling, windswept, once
when there was only my mind

and no other mind. And only at night and when the night broke
into day—and in the day there was actual light.

❧

Sky

is what showed the way

to the New World: the stars commanded *this way*. Oskar,
oh, little son of the sky—son holding the fat baby son's hand

through the snow: we point out the milky way. Oskar, I tell him,

the mind of night and the mind of light, they

brought us to this. Brought us this reciprocal looming unreadable map

we point you toward.

They made us this way.

Kasthaputta Vanhu

SUNU P. CHANDY

"But they came all the way here already,
taking such troubles."

When we left the Chennai orphanage
last August, we left our baby

formula, sweets, diapers, lotion, lice
shampoo and even the travel umbrella
from our handbag. We took in return

only an image of her rocking
herself and a traced outline of her left
foot. The floral pattern on my light green
notebook could not hide ten years
of dismay but now it contained one footstep

towards something possible. My narrow
notebook like the ones made of scraps
from the printing press given for free
to the workers. That season
Mary Oliver worked at the press she said
she only wrote narrow poems.

We had arrived with one pair
of toddler shoes, brown,
size seven, with pink flowers, but much
too large for her tiny feet. I now carried

an accurate drawing of her left
foot throughout Brooklyn, searching
for something small and perfect enough

"Kasthaputta vanhu" (But they came all the way here already, taking such troubles) is a phrase that was repeated several times during a telephone conversation between the orphanage director and the orphanage lawyer while we sat in the orphanage director's office, hearing only her side of the conversation.

that could stand up later in remembrance
as her first pair of shoes. Now, one year
later, a little girl in brown and pink shoes skips
down the subway corridor on her morning
commute from Brooklyn to Manhattan.

Six Days in the Crabapple

MELISSA STEPHENSON

1.

Rocking her to sleep upright to ease the earache
you notice robins by the dozen fill the forty-foot crabapple—
a tree some find hard to believe in. You worry about
the late-season snow, the pressure on her eardrum,
the cold-snap in the forecast. Below zero, it says,
and here they flew all this way gambling on spring.

2.

An engine-seizing cold grips the valley
and you wonder where they're hiding.
Branches stand stark, half-dressed
in last season's red fruit.

3.

Her fever lifts, the valley warms, the birds return.
All Monday they feast. One moment here, another gone—
a lone falcon spinning its head, hunting. Every hour
you check the upstairs window, eyes level
with robins, with falcon, robins, falcon—
a high-stakes dance from which there are few exits.

4.

On the way to the coffee shop you pass a man who sits
every morning in his truck and through binoculars
watches the sky for you-don't-know-what:
elk herds on the mountain, your flock of robins,

a message woven in contrail patterns, weather-mapping
the clouds so he can claim he knew it, knew
it was coming the whole day long.

5.

Dusk and the robins populate the tree—remains
of the fruit now staining the snow a spent amber.
You talk her into eardrops to be sure, tuck her in with a story
about a little girl who survives all predators, seal it with a kiss.
Back at the window you consider the mechanism of instinct
that tells the birds to leave the tree at dark:
wind, scent, dimming light, or magnetic pull?

6.

Stop. Watch it climbing through the window, above
your bank account, your half-broke tooth, over
the man you once loved whole (her father, who
once loved you), over your sleeping child,
the melting snow, stray feathers:
alight on bird-less branches now,
a third-quarter moon rising.

from "Whereas"

LAYLI LONG SOLDIER

WHEREAS her birth signaled the responsibility as mother to teach what it is to be Lakota, therein the question: what did I know about being Lakota? Signaled panic, blood rush my embarrassment. What did I know of our language but pieces? Would I teach her to be pieces. Until a friend comforted, *don't worry, you and your daughter will learn together.* Today she stood sunlight on her shoulders lean and straight to share a song in Diné, her father's language. To sing she motions simultaneously with her hands I watch her *be* in multiple musics. At a ceremony

to honor the Diné Nation's first poet laureate, a speaker explains that each People has been given their own language to reach with. I understand reaching as active, a motion. He offers a prayer and introduction in heritage language. I listen as I reach my eyes into my hands, my hands onto my lap, my lap as the quiet page I hold my daughter in. I rock her back, forward, to the rise of other conversations

about mother tongues versus foster languages, belonging. I connect the dots. I rock in time with references to a philosopher, a master language-thinker who thought of his mother too. Mother-to-child and child-to-mother relationships. But as this philosopher's mother suffered the ill-effects of a stroke he wrote, *I asked her if she was in pain (yes) then where? [. . . she] replies to my question: I have a pain in my mother, as though she were speaking for me, both in my direction and in my place.* His mother, who spoke in his place for his pain and as herself for her own, did this as one-and-the-same. Yet he would propose understanding the word *mother* by what mother is not, the *différance.* Forward, back, I lift my feet

my toes touch ground as I'm reminded of the linguistic impossibility of identity, as if any of us can be identical ever. To whom, to what? Perhaps to Not. I hold my daughter in comfort saying *iyotanchilah michuwintku.* True, I'm never sure how to write our language on the page correctly, the written takes many forms

yet I know she understands through our motion. Rocking, in this country of so many languages where national surveys assert that Native languages are dying. Child-speakers and elder-teachers dwindle, this is public information. But her father and I don't teach in statistics, in this dying I mean. Whereas speaking, itself, is *defiance*—the closest I can come to *différance*. Whereas I confess

these are numbered hours spent responding to a national apology which concerns us, my family. These hours alone to think, without. My hope: my daughter understands wholeness for what it is, not for what it's not, all of it   the pieces;

A Series of Short Stories or Propositions

신 선 영 SUN YUNG SHIN

One by one, the children of the world underwent a metamorphosis. Gates of ivory crushed to dust.

❧

One by one, living people of the world underwent a metamorphosis. Gates of horn polished like glass.

❧

One by one, the dead people of the world began to outnumber the living and the annual games became lopsided. Ribbons trailed from every ankle. A crown of white flowers, petals all asunder . . .

❧

The male calf that was ripped away from his mother, a dairy cow, wept. His mother wept. This was repeated. They never saw each other again. The mother sensed that her son was killed after a long, dry train ride. She felt the squeal of the train wheels against the tracks especially in her left knee. The wet weather of a mother's body.

❧

A girl fell into the river. Her pale blue jeans became dark blue jeans. Her eyes stayed the same color. The color of the past.

❧

At a run-down sperm bank, a centrifuge stopped working properly but they continued to use it anyway. The children that resulted from those sperm felt themselves drawn to the outer edges of things all their lives and never understood why. They could never get far enough from the center. They sought out round rooms and spaces but there were never enough, not even in Greece, where they all ended up, where they all eventually died. They died and the centrifuge was still being used by the indifferent workers at the bank. A cold country, the workers wore mittens inside.

☙

Two bodies in bed felt the shore (or "water" or "surf"?—does the shore lap?) lap upon their limbs. Their bed was captured while they were still on it by the tidal waves. The white sheets upon the bed trailed the bed like a ghost. They were afraid, but happy. Creatures swam like punctuation on a page.

☙

A young boy found a tether and picked it up in his small hand. He liked ropes and things like that. He liked how they could take on any shape and could also lie still and quiet. He followed the tether far into the distance. No one ever saw him again, but he may still be following the tether, perhaps to a kind of maypole in the future.

☙

A group of dogs decided to flee their masters. One was so vain he had to have his nails trimmed and his coat brushed by the maid before he would agree to leave. He brought her the clipper and the brush in his large mouth. She carefully trimmed his black nails that were like buffalo horn and brushed his gray coat until it gleamed in the light. He fell asleep, thinking of his beauty. The other dogs left without him.

☙

There was a lonely priest.

☙

A woman became obsessed with zombie movies. She started making various algorithms and models of epidemiological disasters. She wrote the word "plague" all over her walls, but no one came to look at her beautiful handwriting. Her DVD player nearly broke from playing so many zombie movies, but she coaxed it back to life with some gentle teasing. When the woman eventually died because she forgot to eat or drink, she didn't realize she had died, and neither had anyone else. She died happily ever after, watching her zombie movies and writing the word "plague" over and over again until her walls were covered with solid layers of ink.

❧

A giant office printer ruled a country as its king and its god. People smeared laser jet toner all over their naked bodies and danced around bonfires. Public hangings increased until the printer put a stop to it by grinding up the executioners into pulp for paper. Nobody liked that paper because it was tainted with so much glee. It was like looking at the sun.

❧

One year all the mothers named their newborn babies "Adult."

❧

The alphabet got tired of being abused. It ran away, but not all the letters had legs and feet. Even the one-legged letters hopped away. Some were left behind. There were so many words we couldn't spell anymore. All we had was U, O, C, B, and even those tried to roll away. It was hard to catch them, but what else could we do? R, H, K, X, N, and M were distant memories. Eventually even the old timers couldn't remember them.

❧

In a different version, everything else happened. I was finally at peace.

❧

For one whole decade, it rained inside houses so everyone lived outside their house. They had to look at their neighbors doing everything. If anyone built a house, it immediately began raining in there. The houses recycled the rain, so the streets never flooded. The houses did not disintegrate, but fish and sea life did begin to gather inside. They watched the people go about their business outside. Those prone to melancholy couldn't look inside until the decade was over and the water drained toward the ocean and things went back to normal.

❧

In Hell, all the dead Nazi officers were burned to life.

❧

In Hell, all the wives of the dead Nazi officers continued to scold their Polish maids because the food was overcooked.

❧

One day, all the soldiers broke their guns and buried them deep in the earth. The roots of trees reclaimed them and occasionally you would see a tree with some dark metal sticking out of a branch. Birds landed on them just the same. Over seasons, these exposed pieces rusted and eventually broke into dust.

❧

Over the course of human evolution, we—

❧

Instead of there being two genders, eventually gender became stages, the way a butterfly begins as a pupa, then becomes a caterpillar, then encases itself in a cocoon, growing wings and emerging as a butterfly. Gender became resurrection. Gender became a kind of recycling.

❧

Each soul could bring one thing with them to the Afterlife. They could not bring gender. Some brought their childhoods, however painful. Some brought a single lucid dream. Some brought a memory of music. Some brought their bodies, often carried gently in their arms like a beloved child.

❧

Face transplants became popular later in the century. (Organ donation had become mandatory in the middle of the century.) It never failed to alarm her to come across someone with the face of a dead person. Some people pre-sold their faces on the black market so as to leave their loved ones with a better estate. In the worst cases, people desperate for cash sold their faces while they were still alive. They wore sterile aqueous masks and stayed inside. They used the internet to communicate with others. It wasn't so bad, they said, I wasn't that much to look at before anyway.

In the era of cloning, DNA evidence was no longer enough to convict someone of a crime. So many people had the exact same DNA. The field of forensics exploded as criminology attempted to keep up with the replication trade. A strange side effect of cloning in society was an increase in murders, with primes murdering their clones and clones murdering their primes. It was a mess.

Fathers became irrelevant. Then mothers became irrelevant. Then children became irrelevant. Then humans became irrelevant. Robots didn't consider themselves relevant, exactly, but they knew how to get things done.

Pinocchio enjoyed a tremendous comeback as the story of choice. People couldn't be trusted with real children, so every couple was given a wooden marionette. Many of these marionettes ended up in the municipal trash. But, many escaped. Sometimes you'll think you see one of them in a tree, but then it will turn out to be just a tree (or "branch"?).

Every marionette at first was named Pinocchio and people didn't really like that. Italians liked it, but really nobody else. So people stopped using names but it was illegal to change the name of the marionettes. So people began staying in small groups so they could refer to the different marionettes with hand gestures or phrases such as "this one," or "that one." Small clusters of social groups developed this way.

☙

The marionettes would secretly use the letters of Pinocchio to make names for themselves, names they shared with no one. Late at night you might hear one of them whispering to itself, nochipnoc . . . that has a nice ring to it . . .

☙

The problem with being a marionette was upkeep. Wood needed to be re-sanded, re-stained, re-painted, re-lacquered. Limbs broke and new ones had to be made on a lathe.

☙

The good thing was that you could take parts from three broken marionettes to repair a newer one. The old ones were burned. People covered their eyes and ears during the burning, as if there might be screaming, but there never was. Not during the burning, anyway.

Two Glasses of Milk

TERI ELLEN CROSS DAVIS

If I were to leave them
two glasses of milk,
don't write about that,
write about the napkin
the perfect triangle tucked
around the circle of glass,
the absorbed condensation.

If I were to leave them
two glasses of milk, it would be
the tension of motherhood
and career, poet and wife
pulling like teeth at my
extended nipples until I was
greedily consumed in silence.

If I were to leave them
two glasses of milk,
even across my tombstone
would be the words:
daughter, wife, mother.
Identities like anchors,
so heavy I would carry
them even after death.

Our Family on the Run

BRENDA SHAUGHNESSY

Everything organized around Cal in his wheelchair. He can't walk and I can't carry him far. We'd have the wheelchair van, as long as we could find gas. Simone in the side seat, Craig and me in the front.

Maybe spray paint a Super Soaker metallic silver to look like a real weapon?

Load the car up with cans of enteral food for Cal's G-tube. Maybe a six-week supply, plus a go-backpack full of cans, extensions, spare Mic-Key button. Three days of food for the rest of us. We'll find water.

Sleeping in the front seats, taking turns on watch. Simone curled up next to the gas can and ziplock of batteries / cords / chargers, with her one stuffed animal we have to worry about something happening to, her only toy.

And what if we lose the car? Running on the side road to—
Pennsylvania / airport / Atlantic / evacuation center / relocation camp / as yet unknown. Trying to buy a blow-up raft for four people. Can't take the wheelchair.

Our stack of euros to buy four plane tickets: can't take the wheelchair.

On foot, trying to get to a friend's country home, promise of a bedroom. No way to call the friend for directions. A compass one of the kids got at a birthday party wound up under a car seat. Lucky.

Lucky, too, Simone can walk—though she gets tired and I'd want to hoist her on my back if I didn't have to save my energy to carry Cal when Craig's legs give way, his back out.

Cal, four foot six and sixty pounds of tween, who must be carried if we somehow lose that wheelchair. Or the wheelchair breaks, or it is stolen, or gets a flat tire, or rusts.

It's red, a color Cal chose by smiling when we said "red" in a list of colors. No expression when we said blue, green, black, purple, or pink. Big smile when we said red. He has his choice and he made it.

How strange that the color of his wheelchair ever mattered enough to anyone to offer him that handful of options.

Simone is hungry. I give her a Clif bar (that twenty-four pack I bought for rushed mornings) and she drops half of it on the dirt road, which is covered in, what, bone dust or atomized drywall?

She grabs what she dropped and stuffs it into her mouth before I can stop her. Why would I stop her?

The side of the road is the well-known gutter of desperation always included in stories about wars where many people have to move on foot to the next terrible place.

No matter what the emergency, whenever people are forced to flee you find, piece by piece, how their understanding of their situation changed.

If you read the stories, you're supposed to find abandoned photo albums, suitcases, babies. The useless things cut out by survival's swift knife. Dead weight, long gone.

You never find food, bottled water, working flashlights, live batteries, shortwave radios. It's true, what all those stories said, it turns out.

Eventually out of water and arms shredded, I carry Cal, Craig carries me, and Simone carries us all. Almost seven years old, she is so strong and has some Clif bars stuffed in a bag. The notebook with all our information is long lost.

She knows where she's going. How does she know that? She runs ahead and carries us, her heart pounding and breaking with the weight and strain of all of us in there.

ƒ = [(*root*) (*future*)]

VANESSA ANGÉLICA VILLARREAL

year [0]
*Matrilineal = repeat
∄ ("Cycle", "Inherit", DOES NOT EXIST)

[0=Carmen]
blooming ranch fields a throat
packed with cotton no choice
but to marry her eldest off to
the hoofbeaten storm

[0=Angelica]
escape the hoofbeaten storm
escape the garnet-eyed doctor
escape the stillborn country
that pummels you to rags

[0=Silvia]
ENGLISH SYNONYMS FOR FUTURE
escape; amnesty; green card; possibility;
dream; I promise; I will; I do; pregnant;
labor; indebted; hospitalized; sole; provider;
burden; loan; insufficient; interest;

[0=Vanessa]
witness this pattern, now cycling into me;
again lost eddies of time lost again I submerge
my body in the river of unclaimed memory
swim again to its cervix and speak into the sea:
I did everything I was supposed to do, and still, an
unbroken line of broken lines;

[1=Joaquin]
If someone is going to make it out of this dream alive, let it be
you, unbraiding from me. Let it be that this cord, its arcing line,
when viewed from above, is an infinite field. And let the field open
for you like a bell, its bend veined with a lace of new stars. And let each
new star echo on earth as a blossom, bursting from the black so
that you, born from this blooddark grief, marbled with error, can still
be perfect. Let every good beast carry you in its eye, open with wild
knowing. And let every sagging telephone line carry my voice to you when I'm
gone, when you're lonely, or scared, and in a sleepsoft drift, you'll think
you hear me in the kitchen. And yes, there we are again, reflected in
the bend of the steel spoon, the milk still spinning as we lick off the chocolate;
and there we are again, in the rust-burnt dusk, embers whirling off the
mountainside, the last sight we'll have of an ocean; and yes, I'm sorry,
I am so, so sorry—what else could I have done to stop the cell from splitting

PRIME MERIDIAN OF UNIVERSAL TIME, ROYAL OBSERVATORY 0° 00:00:00

FUTURELESS PAST

0°, 00:00:0

<

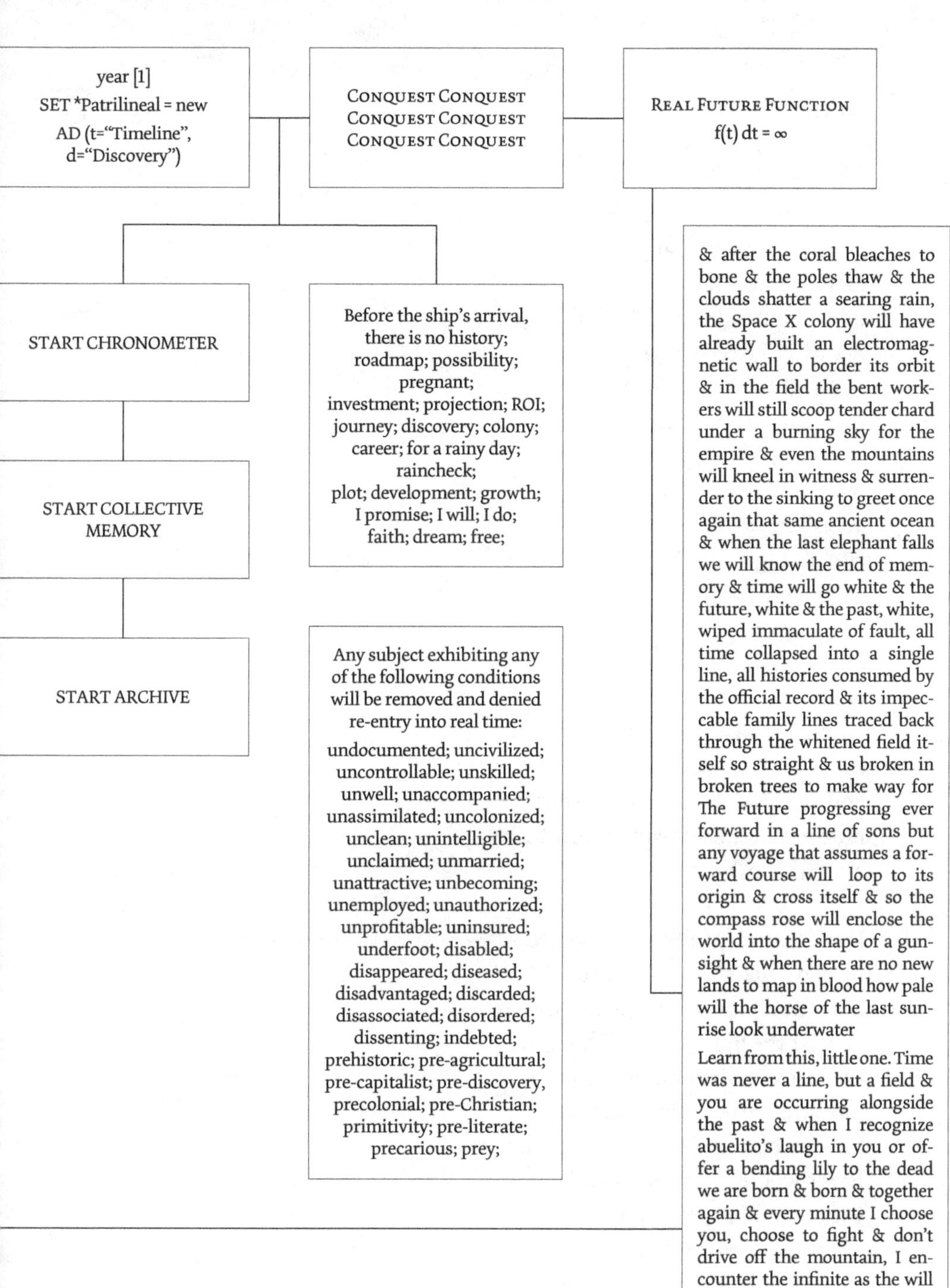
year [1]
SET *Patrilineal = new
AD (t="Timeline",
d="Discovery")
CONQUEST CONQUEST
CONQUEST CONQUEST
CONQUEST CONQUEST
REAL FUTURE FUNCTION
f(t) dt = ∞
START CHRONOMETER
START COLLECTIVE
MEMORY
START ARCHIVE
Before the ship's arrival,
there is no history;
roadmap; possibility;
pregnant;
investment; projection; ROI;
journey; discovery; colony;
career; for a rainy day;
raincheck;
plot; development; growth;
I promise; I will; I do;
faith; dream; free;
Any subject exhibiting any
of the following conditions
will be removed and denied
re-entry into real time:
undocumented; uncivilized;
uncontrollable; unskilled;
unwell; unaccompanied;
unassimilated; uncolonized;
unclean; unintelligible;
unclaimed; unmarried;
unattractive; unbecoming;
unemployed; unauthorized;
unprofitable; uninsured;
underfoot; disabled;
disappeared; diseased;
disadvantaged; discarded;
disassociated; disordered;
dissenting; indebted;
prehistoric; pre-agricultural;
pre-capitalist; pre-discovery,
precolonial; pre-Christian;
primitivity; pre-literate;
precarious; prey;
& after the coral bleaches to bone & the poles thaw & the clouds shatter a searing rain, the Space X colony will have already built an electromagnetic wall to border its orbit & in the field the bent workers will still scoop tender chard under a burning sky for the empire & even the mountains will kneel in witness & surrender to the sinking to greet once again that same ancient ocean & when the last elephant falls we will know the end of memory & time will go white & the future, white & the past, white, wiped immaculate of fault, all time collapsed into a single line, all histories consumed by the official record & its impeccable family lines traced back through the whitened field itself so straight & us broken in broken trees to make way for The Future progressing ever forward in a line of sons but any voyage that assumes a forward course will loop to its origin & cross itself & so the compass rose will enclose the world into the shape of a gunsight & when there are no new lands to map in blood how pale will the horse of the last sunrise look underwater
Learn from this, little one. Time was never a line, but a field & you are occurring alongside the past & when I recognize abuelito's laugh in you or offer a bending lily to the dead we are born & born & together again & every minute I choose you, choose to fight & don't drive off the mountain, I encounter the infinite as the will to survive
REAL TIME

Fallible Beasts

EMARI DIGIORGIO

In the dream, my daughter,
just three, peers at the edge
of the hippo tank and I'm holding
her with the type of grip
most mothers use when hoisting
their sunscreen-slick toddler,
as she leans in, squealing,
but then her weight shifts
and she tips into the tank
and it's high enough that I
cannot swing my leg over
the concrete bulwark, nothing
at my feet to stand on,
which is why I was holding her
in the first place. Their teeth
are not tea-stained marshmallows
and I'm spared the sound, a silent
horror film, this dream, a nightmare
another mother's lived through.

I read the story of the boy mauled
by two jaguars at the Little Rock Zoo,
how the crew used fire extinguishers
to blast the big cats back, though
the black one had bitten the boy's
foot and the yellow his nape.
If we're looking for a causal chain,
here's where Harambe goes down
with a thud. *Oh, Harambe, we love
you get up*. Beautiful beast batting
his eyes and that intelligent stride.

When a team of scientists
and photographers and artists
goes into the Antarctic to study

its majesty, they return from the day's
trek to discover a polar bear
breaking into a tent. They don't kill
the bear because already he's eaten
all of the food (straight through
aluminum cans), exposed film,
dragged an air mattress outside
and shred it to prayer flags.
One man's wounded tone,
as if to say *I trusted you, wild thing,*

and you have abused my trust.
Dear human, even if you've paid
for the land, the single-story house,
you rent this plot from ants. And what
would Harambe's mother, Kayla,
dead a dozen years now, a gas leak
at the Gladys Porter Zoo, what would
she do? Majestic in her own way,
how she stroked her two-year-old's
shoulders and scolded him
in a terribly familiar timbre.

I'd bet my own clapboard house
that she'd kill any man she thought
a threat. You, mother, standing
at the edge of the simulated rainforest,
your fear as real as the scrub grass
at your feet. All mothers
have failed. Sometimes it's a bit
of fiberglass insulation spun
like carnival cotton candy. Five fingers
caught in a car door. My own child bit
by a beach restaurant's pet parrot.
I watched it. She was pretending,
as children do, that she was cooking,

and when she offered the parrot,
high in the rafters, a small plate

of crushed shells and sticks,
he swooped down and chawed
her meaty shin breaking it into blood
bright as the bird's back. The owners
squawked and my daughter cried.
They didn't kill the bird, but each
time we returned, he was caged,
and I was sorry for this, too.

There are things that don't seem
possible, until they are. If we're
taking sides, I'm taking this mother's,
not because I'm a mother who's
failed, or the child of a mother
who's failed too–all of our palm-sized
and glacier failures lined up,
reclaiming the word, which comes
from the Latin *fallere*, which means
to deceive: We want to believe
we can do better, but we too
are wild, fallible beasts.

Recognition

SASHA WEST

How many storms out of season—a river
rerouted, a current of goods, swelling—but trying
to act normal, all around, people in a kind of

normalcy. Storms made better footage than a slow
starvation. That summer, subway tile everywhere,
and chevrons. Friends dressed well, read well, we

ate farm-to-table meals on one staged set or another—a kind
of illness this swaddled edge of miniature wealth, an illness
not to enjoy this playacting—I kept my mind away

from others the way a sick person doesn't
shake hands, the TV showed us what we couldn't
afford, then stores knocked down workers until

we could, and we had private traumas, deaths
and abuse, assault and grief, enough to keep us
blindered, muddling, in sorrow, enough

not to look too closely—we had two cars, a fridge,
a washing machine, were told we were what the whole
world wanted—have you tried the cold brew coffee?

the activated charcoal cocktail? We had children
who seared joy into us—and toil—and wrote dead
letters to the government, made signs, marched

against the violences we could see—all of it filled
time the way a life does, expanded if we gave it
space, where would those future bodies

go? Where could be quiet enough to imagine
our children's limbs, neighbor's house
in wind we'd never seen? What deserted mall

could be big enough to house the imagined
carcasses of the dying-off animals? Guilt obscures
grief, consolation burns from the inside. I tried to

enlarge my mind the way I'd eaten my pregnant
belly into expansion, swallowing each day more
facts and still I could not contain the entire

ice shelf, the size overwhelmed, the numbers
overwhelmed, at least I could put my body in a storm
to be dwarfed—my heart gulped up the graph lines,

the exponential increase. I put the two boys drowned
in mud inside my daughter's body, then the refugees
in tents, the accumulating genocide, growing speed until

none of them seemed real, until even she disappeared
when I left the room, every time I arrived at the edge
of what the human mind can do, I went back and forth

across the threshold where humans became data, trying
to keep more bodies living in the numbers, but
the disintegration spread, I could feel humans

extending as far back as my imagination could go, but
blurred and flickering forward—and I had made her
to come here and stand in the middle of what

our species had made. Who were the Greek kings
who put their daughters out to be sacrificed? I had
brought her out of my body, had her umbilical

cord cut to bind her to the rock, the mast, the world.

More Moon

KIM-AN LIEBERMAN

Moon! calls the baby, *more moon!*
Awake with language tonight, she finds
moons rising ubiquitous—
streetlamps, porchlights, storefronts.

The sidewalk a galaxy,
the whole city stippled with silver,
with toys and spoons dropped again and again
to see if gravity sticks.

Down our late path, she cries
moon, moon, moon! and each time
the meaning turns new:

how small I am, how large the night

pearl upon pearl in my satchel of words

as you wane to nothing, I learn to be

Someday she will know light from light—
for now, let her world shimmer.
I lull her to sleep, and then myself,
whispering *moon, moon:*

as I wane to nothing, you learn to be

how lush-spun the velvet on valley and field

trail of gems, brightly tipped and dreaming

Inevitable

MAHOGANY L. BROWNE

When I dropped my 12-year-old off at her first
homecoming dance, I tried not to look

at her newly developed breasts, all surprise and alert
in their uncertainty. I tried not to imagine her

mashed between a young man's curiousness
and the gym's sweaty wall. I tried not to picture

her grinding off beat / on time to the rhythm
of a dark manchild, the one who whispered

"you are the most beautiful girl in brooklyn"
his swag so sincere, she'd easily mistaken him for a god.

Extrapolating Motherhood

KRISTA FRANKLIN

Outside, at two in the morning
I say "motherfucker" for the Colombians
to teach them to curse the way only
an American can. *Drop the "R,"* I tell
these men who roll R's as pretty as some
of my friends roll joints. We are five different kinds
of drunk, high off the promise of summer
and a white, pregnant moon. I think of Paulette,
years ago at the Christmas Party, newly
pregnant with a boy named Gabriel,
pissed off at everything she could not
have: the bottle of vodka the Russian broke out,
the stinky mushrooms sneakily circulating.
This is the story Gabriel will never know;
the first night he stood in the doorway
of his mother's true nature. How she departed
abruptly to grapple with his arrival. How many
women never speak of this.

A DJ leans in my passenger's side window
to spin a yarn bout Babymama Number One,
how she'd show up at his gigs swoll up with
the best track he'll ever lay or play, and perch
up on top the speakers. This was supposed
to tip me about how wild she was. Forgive my
vulgarity: when a woman pushes a person
out her pussy, it transforms her. This is what
I'm telling you. It's not always good.
When I was a girl, my mother made this clear,
feeding every child in the neighborhood,
dragging every unwanted kid off the street.
There are so many children, but mothers
are scarce. Or scarcely sane, plowing their
seed with every insecurity they dream up. There
are multiple narratives to every story. Why not
those of mothers?

I marvel. These women who defrag to DNA,
expand like magic, quell wails with their breasts.
I don't begrudge that. Nor the exquisiteness
of a six-month-old cheek, the charisma of a toothless
grin. Being a kid is more appealing
than having one. Only a woman who no one calls
"Mama" should stand outside at two in the morning
teaching how to say "motherfucker."
These are vulgarities one should not
reproduce. Some folks don't get that,
and have kids anyway. It's one of the reasons
my mother fed them. There are times
those children and I lock eyes. Being a child
like them, I cannot tell you what they tell me.

The Excavation

JENN GIVHAN

My 8-yr-old daughter is teaching me
how to live with myself
after 34yrs in this body I can finally

split myself in two & marvel that now I pass
the Bechdel test.
What I've let men scavenge—

my collarbones, femurs, the fleshy pads
of my inner thighs, bitemarks
butterflying from the clotted cream

that cornmeal death has made
of my skin—has given
way to blood

poisoning.   I haven't done much but get dumped
by one & tell the other to stop raping
me when I'm dreamcumming

& he finally after 13yrs together & a year
of divorce
understands a sleeping body moaning

is not consent. & while he's had to learn
truths he should've learned as a boy
I too chart a map to my unlearning.

I rewatch the filmstrips of my girlhood
with my girl & she covers her face at kissy scenes
& very practically, very kindly but firmly

lifecoaches the girls/women
You are worth so much more than you know
& finally I hear from the gift of my womb

what my mother never
taught me. My daughter transforms the desert
of my memory—peels the spines

from the cacti, fashions me a crown
that asks Who were you when you weren't blooming only
for boys? & I recall the night-

blooming cereus, whose bats fly hundreds of miles
one night of the year to sustain themselves
on the sweet nectar, & how many

mornings I missed, how many
dark things I emptied myself for. My daughter
is a graveyard by which I mean ripe

for rebirthing. She pulls me from the beds
I've buried & tells me
if she is wise it's because I've taught her

by which she means
I've held myself deep within
myself all along.

I've plucked bones & swapped
for jackrabbit for woodrat for javelina. O tusks
o glorious horns

I've borne
from daughter, from the un-
mothered loam.

Nocturne

ANGELA NARCISO TORRES

Awake beneath an onyx sky you crack the blinds, inhale
night's fading ink. The air is your mother's breath on your skin,
the only steeple is the church of palms in the neighbor's yard

dropping vermilion fruit on the grass. On another coast,
everyone you know is sleeping except for a boy you love.
In his body ticks a clock that matches yours. Darkness seeps

from the blades of palmetto the way water leaves your fingers
after a bath. To see the darkness, one must look darkly. Hours later,
this boy will feed his cat, perform his daily ministrations

like a mother. What is parenting but a prayer for one's young.
Outside, the white ibis of dawn unfurls the potted mint,
its ribbons of scent. Son, your shadow lives in my eyes.

Words in the Air: On Audio Drafting

EMARI DIGIORGIO

I'm doing it now: talking to myself, earbuds in and voice memo on, as I set out down the macadam road. I'm not quite sure how long I'll walk or talk, but I often have some destination in mind, an idea for a poem, a memory I want to turn over like a stone, to see what lives beneath.

Right now, I'm thinking and talking about this essay, about the ways my process has changed as a not-quite-new-anymore mother. I'm trying to remember the first audio draft. I'd look it up if I used Dropbox then, but I lost that new mama laptop to a roadside robbery in Nicaragua.

What I am absolutely certain of is how hard it is to type with an infant at your breast, even with the My Brest Friend© strapped around your torso. My own milk-drunk daughter would bob beneath my hands as I typed. A comic sight as I balanced my elbows above her bouncing head and prayed she'd stay asleep a little longer so that I could finish whatever thought evaded me.

In the days before my daughter was born, I could sit for hours with a cup of tea. I could start with a line or image and spend hours turning it over. I could draft at my leisure because I had the day; even if I had plans, I had no one who needed me immediately, no real interruptions, beyond the cat pawing to get on my lap or laptop. Nothing really needed me. So those hours were swallowed up by writing, yes, and reading, but sometimes social media and the rabbit hole of research on the internet.

But then she arrived. She slept, if I was lucky, in two hour clips all nights, and I did not exist for myself or my writing at all. I was feeding her on one breast, burping her, feeding her on the other, changing her diaper, putting her down, pumping excess milk, washing the pump, and sometimes she'd be back up or she never slept. Sometimes I needed to feed myself.

Anyone who has had a young one knows this comic conveyor belt of need. I had not forgotten about writing; in fact, I had done quite the opposite. Right before my daughter was born, I had intentionally taken an online workshop with Ada Limón. I had treated myself to this class as a birthday/new mother's gift. During my pregnancy, I also decided that I wanted to write the poems I had been avoiding in some way, to write into my own trauma and survival. The thought of bringing a girl-child into the world created an urgency to speak truth. To be the mother I wanted to be, I had to be the writer I wanted to be, too.

However, after she arrived, I don't think I read anything besides the baby sleep manual, a book on introducing foods, and whatever short articles (or poems) I might read on my phone on the toilet. I remember longing to return to the drafts I had just written. I'd think, *if I could just have an hour*. But if I had an hour or four, I really needed to sleep to burn off the fog of baby brain. I needed a shower, to cut my own nails. I needed quiet.

Six months later, when I returned to work in September, I discovered that at least I could draft in the car. Using the voice memo application on my iPhone, I could talk through an idea. I had already learned that if I sat at my computer for thirty minutes, those were thirty minutes I could have done something else, instead of the three lines I squeaked out. But here, when I was already doing something else—a task that was using one part of my brain, driving—surely I could use another part of my brain, the part I'd use for talking. It was a two-for-one, and now I could use those cherished thirty minutes at my laptop to transcribe the twenty-minute audio file, and I'd have a whole page (or two!) of text.

Clearly, the first part of audio drafting is efficiency. As a mother / teacher / human, I had very little time, and full disclosure, I'm a Capricorn with a tremendous urge for productivity. However, I also know as a writer that if I have a mass of text on the screen, I can find more than three lines worth saving. In fact, in any given audio draft I'll discover whole stanzas or a dominant image, or I'll have located some rhythms and the first sense of "organic form," as Levertov calls it. Audio drafting offers an onramp into poems in my new time-crunched life. But it did something else, too. It freed my inner editor, the one who would revise a phrase or idea so much that it would stymie me, and it might not even permit me to explore that terrain.

Just talking, releasing the words into the air, like I am now, surrounded by the thick scent of honeysuckle and clover in eastern Tennessee, where I'm spending two weeks at a writing residency, feels less permanent. I can revise a sentence in the moment, but I don't lose the original. Instead, the recording shows my amendment. When I listen to transcribe, I can hear the first thought and how the immediate second or third thoughts modified the phrasing or ideas in these ways, and sometimes this thinking is exactly what the poem is about.

I've kept this audio drafting process even now at this residency where I have endless hours to myself, where I don't need to multitask. I know I am more likely to provide an honest interrogation of a difficult memory or topic; I'm more likely to play with words and sounds without just thinking they're silly. This process invites a sense of play and freedom that I had written out of myself.

In my real life, I can also break drafting into manageable chunks. If an audio file is eighteen minutes long, I can pick a twenty-minute block to transcribe it. I choose to transcribe, instead of using an app, because I like to hear those pauses, to note where I was thinking and breathing hard. I like to return to the place on the trail where I may have noticed a butterfly or pet a dog because it gets me back into the original moment of composition, that raw energy of drafting. I also can pause it because new images or language might open up to me as I'm listening to my voice mull over these ideas.

Once I have that mass of text, if I have more than the requisite transcription time, I can start to look for compressed language and music. I can admire some of the phrasing that I might have dismissed initially. As I identify these early patterns, I can determine where the poem might want to go.

For me, being a parent has involved split attention and doing things in pieces or parts, so audio drafting has saved my writing. Nearly all of the poems in my second book, *Girl Torpedo*, were written this way. If I'm honest, I don't remember how I used to spend so much time at my computer, almost waiting for the poem to arrive whole.

Each time I set out on these audio walks and drives, I don't know what I'm going to discover. I've returned to memories I didn't know I carried; I've uncovered uncomfortable truths about myself. When I look up from the road, I remember that I am part of this brutal and beautiful world and there is so much else beyond my life. I don't think that audio drafting is the only way to have a writing practice as a parent, but it's one that I've found practical and sustainable. It allows me to not give up any of the things I'm split between.

War Songs: Mothering through Climate Change

SASHA WEST

"Recognition" is a poem with a war inside of it.

I came to motherhood having spent a disproportionate amount of time studying poems about wars: Poems by men who fought in World War I and World War II, some of whom swallowed whole the jingoism, some of whom swallowed horror. The ones breathed by survivors of Hiroshima, trying to explain what it was to lose a city, layers of flesh in a flash of light. The ones bled out by the witnesses of the Holocaust and its aftermath, breaking syntax to speak of corpses stacked like kindling. The ones by veterans and protestors of Vietnam, dismantling in real time ideas of war as dignity or justice.

No one questioned the way war could be a lens. Though the writers were unlike me—mostly male, elsewhere in history and geography—both my teachers and I understood there to be value in experiences that move your body into a different kind of knowing. It was the strangeness of the lives we didn't share that widened our own. No one expected war poems to be universal or relatable. (We hoped they wouldn't be.) What was valuable was how they let us see what happens at the edges of humanity.

Birth took me to the edge of humanity. My body wasn't in jeopardy—though I had never seen so much of my own blood. But the boundary my culture had worked so hard to create between my body and the body of other animals started to wear away. An umbilical cord had tethered me to civilization. It could be severed.

Before motherhood, I had seen birth's strangest experiences whittled down to tropes: the water breaks, there are screams and a team of mostly strangers, a baby howls and is quickly made a swaddled, clean baby, put into arms. We are quickly returned to the known.

The afterbirth was elided—the wait between delivering the baby and the placenta—this strange object, this disposable organ that had been my daughter's companion. When the obstetrician showed me the unfamiliar mass of it, she might as well have been showing me a new species of jellyfish my body had made, animal and alien, flesh and fleeing. My body had grown an organ to feed this little animal that came from me. I was species, phylum, taxonomy.

"Recognition," a poem by Sasha West, appears on page 191 of this volume.

I'd been through other rites of passage: graduations, a marriage ceremony, funerals. In them, I was like other humans, sure—a part of a community, sometimes. But parenthood was the first place I felt the communal experience radiate out in an embodied way. I see other parents with younger children and feel again in my body what it is to chase a toddler through an airport, have the milk let down when the baby suckles. I am inside the body of strangers. The passage was visceral and changed my cells.

There's probably a neurohormonal reason for this or a way that visceral connection gives our animal an evolutionary advantage. But birth made me most wild in form and function—an animal among fellow species. Our previous wild life was not far buried in my skin.

This doppelganger space didn't stop with humans. I felt how close I was as a species to grooming my daughter's hair with my mouth. (Thus the trope of a mother's spit on a handkerchief to clean a dirty face? Someone understands we try to make the cloth our tongue.)

Watching an otter on its mother's belly, the weight I felt on my body was my daughter's over my lungs and liver. She'd inherited the instinct to cover the animal you sleep on with a limb, a head, a haunch. Watching the lion's paw batting away her cub was the gesture I made in frustration when my daughter's play got too wild. Watching the pangolin's grip on its mother's tail, I felt my daughter curled around my arm after a nightmare. I saw my limbs in the elephant gathering its child back to a body with a trunk. The animals, the other humans, and I wore each other's parenting bodies.

I shed the organs and shape I'd grown for her and milked the calcium from my bones for her food. Which is to say, motherhood was a lens that remade my sense of the physical world. Also, the temporal. Motherhood changed the way my mind ranged across the world, its future. My daughter was born the same year the Intergovernmental Panel on Climate Change (IPCC) stepped up their predictions to include sea level rise, mass crop death. Or she was born in one of the years their predictions became more dire. I started to catalogue what was coming. The changes sped. My knowledge deepened.

I hadn't been unengaged before. I had cared so much—I thought—that I wasn't ready for the way a body can push knowledge into the viscera in that cracked open, sleepless space of our first year. Before I cared about climate change because I moved through land, loved animals, imagined humans into disaster. But now I could extend my actual body into the future in a different way through her flesh. I was putting a single face on what the future would do to a person. I had made the face.

The expanse of my care was force-gathered in a single point. She was what pierced and where worry called me. She was the focal point of my imagination. Before I had a child, I lived in the illusion that I could care about the future for all of us. Her birth revealed the lie, that my body felt care about people in concentric circles. Why did I need real flesh to feel the future?

This searing care meant something about the future, but it also portended the present. I edged up against what happens when we put one set of humans above another. Meanwhile, I watched the country turn its fear full-force toward that impulse; I watched the long-unfolding rhetoric, hoarding, and caging that follow treating that concentric impulse as anything other than a starting point. If the salience of my family was animal, I wanted civilization, something beyond the shadow fear. So, there was an embodied animal-ness that felt right to claim after its long elision, and another kind of non-thinking, in-group animal-ness it felt vital to resist.

Other lives came into sharper view through my daughter. I could run her through them. (It's not fair, she shouldn't be a puppet.) It was disappointing to find as a bodily truth that I couldn't make all lenses into the future scenarios equal. Another human should be visible for their very distinctness, the very ways their being is not me, has nothing to do with me. When Natalie Diaz visited the university where I teach, she talked about her distrust of empathy, predicated as it is on the idea that for us to feel something for someone else, we must first move their experience through our own body. So even that understanding is limited to our self. Even in empathy the other person isn't real.

I agree with her. And here I am, deeply partial. The paradox became: here is my deeper, more embodied care for others, because the world radiates out through my daughter.

Hence the poetics of motherhood as a lens into contradictions, inadequacies, clarity.

Poetry has long been a way to investigate these kinds of quarrels with the self. Poetry is an art form that welcomes paradox and departure, elisions and the unsolvable. How well its form fits motherhood's function.

Contemporary poets get to keep every way that other writers have cracked open motherhood—from its tenderness to its violence, from its expansion to its diminishment. We also get to continue the work of writers like Lorde, Rich, and Clifton, who show how being fully inside motherhood opens a new lens for looking at our negotiations with the social and political world. They understood well that parenting under certain historical moments, certain institutions, was akin to being a foot soldier in a larger conflict. You see only a small slice of action that is the lens into the whole.

In parenthood, the quarrel is also with all of civilization. Parents become the gate through which civilization enters the child. We are the guardians of culture, but also the carriers of its contaminations. If I give my daughter the Greek myths, I give her a world full of sexual assault, power grabs, great manners, brilliant transformations, and wars. I give her a world built on sacrifice for those in power. I prepare the way for capitalism and totalitarianism. If I give her the wrong forms of the world, the ones that have allowed tragedies to unfold, she will have to break them to leave.

But caregivers are also the first act of imagination our culture has. When I tell my daughter the story of the world, I can remake it. Later the world's voice takes over, but we get a chance to first make our beautiful argument for what is and what should be. We get a chance through our revisions to shift, slowly, what is. Here I am teaching her the forms and content of the world. What are the forms of knowing, the ways of speaking, that will make them visible?

Poems are invested in meaning-making. The poem becomes a lens for examining the truth of biology and its inadequacies, where my body has led my mind. Stalin relied on the fact that a single death is a tragedy, a million deaths a statistic. How can the poem be a tool for reversing this erasure? In this tiny laboratory of my mindheart, she is the site of investigation: how I can re-see the human relationship to that which is nature and to that what we have called human nature? The struggle I feel in myself is a microcosm of the flaws that led us here.

The spaces that make us not more human but more humane often come after the lie is revealed. For instance, once unconscious bias is tracked, its visibility becomes the way we fight institutionalized racism trying to make sleeper agents of us. Naming is the first step to escaping the mistakes of our species.

The speaker in "Recognition" fails to break the mind's limits of perception. She's thrown back on her human inability to imagine numbers, the limit of the brain despite trying so hard to get out of it. Maybe in naming failure, we make a space for someone else to be better than this. The end of the poem is a reckoning. The failing already has a human cost.

If humans are story-making creatures, what we tell each other is our psychological reckoning. Healing from trauma as a culture will need story-making activity. We might subvert the old idea of having children as producing soldiers for a country and instead think of the meanings we produce as being soldiers toward something other, more livable and true.

I didn't know I'd have to still earn the space to write out of motherhood. I thought the space was well cleared by those before me. A friend posted a poem from the same project as "Recognition," with a line "What could be wilder than the body of a mother?" Someone in the comment thread asked: "I don't know: maybe American sentences?"

The poem wasn't asking what could be wilder in language or culture or experience. Before my daughter, my body had a different kind of freedom. Before the sleeplessness and the balancing of work/writing/parenting, my mind had a different kind of daily range. (The freedoms of mind and syntax—oh, I had those, they ruled me.) I meant how close the body becomes in motherhood to wilderness, to that which we call not human, not civilized. I meant it was my lens into what early humans knew. It was my lens into the great lie I drank from the bones of my culture.

I'm not interested in defending the poem, which didn't arrive at that for this reader. While the comment might have arisen from a general mistrust of the oracular voice—after all, we spent so much time breaking its monolithic hegemony down—it was also a way of saying I shouldn't be asserting things. That's never happened to other poems, where the speaker spoke from other locations, asserted equally personal things. I'm interested in the assumption that the mother could only speak in the poem if her experience was all experiences, if her thoughts were all thoughts.

Writing teaches us that the specific is a lens into the general. No reader expects a soldier's experience to be all experiences. Why must a mother's? If we want absolute relatability, we render the individual voice silent. We never learn what each edge of experience has to teach us.

There's violence in the question, submerged, because we submerge the violences in our lives. We teach our children to place a partition between the sweet animals we give them stuffed effigies of or read to them about in books and the meat we purchase on the Styrofoam trays. We partition their party favors and stocking toys from the great garbage patch in the ocean. We partition the wood we burn for s'mores and the endless pages of scribbles from the deforestation that allows the play. The partition allows us to stay sane—or is it the biggest mark of our insanity?

The violence I do to the planet, I do to my daughter.

The beauty of a poem is its porousness and contradictions. In a poem, the lens can widen until one cannot look away. The poem can contain the war.

If I Admit Who I Am, Who Will I Become?

JORDAN RICE

1.

After decades of silence and months of therapy, I stood in a mostly empty parking lot on the far side of Michigan, staring at the words GENDER CLINIC on a sign in front of an office building at the outer perimeter of a shopping mall. I'd been driving since before dawn, was rushed and sick from too much coffee and six months of coming out to those closest to me. At the end of each of those conversations, someone I loved, usually sitting alone in an office many states south, realized by turns that the person they'd known by the body I'd been when we last said goodbye was never coming home. When the alarm went off that morning my wife stayed in bed, warm, quietly watching me get ready, looking as worried as I was at everything before us. Then it was time, and yes, I promised, I'd drive safely and be home soon, and I love you. Only this life. This one. You too.

2.

This might be the happiest I ever saw you, my mother is saying as she holds a picture of me at five, sitting next to an apple tree in my grandfather's orchard, wearing my uncle's USMC flight helmet. The same age then as I am now, he piloted helicopters the size of small houses, and while training, occasionally flew over his father's farm in western North Carolina, slowing above our tobacco fields and apple trees, tilting the Sikorsky slightly to the left or right. The notepad half under my thigh there in the picture, though, that's what I'd like to point out now, because that was the first day I tried writing anything. My grandmother kept the poem, but told me when I last saw her, that she liked my old work more than what I'm writing now.

3.

The nurse was the calmest person in the room. Then the sudden woosha-woosha and a small screen lit up. Instant recognition. At the end of the first trimester, there in black and gray fractals, was the outline of a head, the pearly curvature of backbone, a small but clearly defined arm raised toward the mouth. My wife laughed, and the image flickered, the small form before us fluttering up, settling back. The nurse switched on the heart rate monitor: 152 beats a minute. Like a marathon runner! my father said the night we broke our news to him, after he calmed down, quit pounding the kitchen table with his fist, his voice a roar through static seven hundred miles away: *That's good! That's good!*

4.

For the first thirty years of my life, I escaped my body most through writing, which became the most recognizable and livable space I knew. But what I've gained from this process of transition, of slowly growing into another self, remains mostly interior. I smile more. I smile.

5.

My son stirs in his nursery. Soon he'll cry, and after some milk, and without ever really having opened his eyes, he'll curl against my chest like every night of his life so far, and snore, and at some point start to laugh from his dream. If nowhere else, it must be said here, I think, that the body cannot and does not matter at such times.

Visibly transgender, somewhere between male and female, however I appear to anyone, but especially to my son, it is first as his parent, second as comfort, and each night as he sleeps, his guardian, the only wakeful person in our house, as I read, write, staying up on purpose, sore armed, sore of chest, often with a cramp in one leg or the other, our son the constant flickering presence on the monitor, until some time near dawn I place him in our bed, where he scrawls his body between his mother and me, until his head rests at my shoulder, his feet at her stomach, each of us then lastingly and only ourselves.

Confetti Time

MELISSA STEPHENSON

I'm a solo parent to two young children, and my writing process revolves around the pockets of time between grocery shopping, dinner fixing, gymnastics carpool, and doctor appointments. All these interruptions—no matter how lovely or mundane—fracture my focus. Three hours divided into ten short writing sessions over three days is not the same as three solid hours of sustained attention. Years ago, I happened upon a phrase that captures the fragmented nature of my days: "confetti time"—my biggest muse and my greatest challenge.

When my kids were two and five, I returned to writing after a four-year hiatus. I drafted memoir shorts at top speed in hopes that I might get down the bones of a piece before naps ended or baths began. Once I had a draft, I knew I could circle back and revise. Soon, the memoir shorts piled up. In a couple years, I realized I'd accrued over one hundred pages of a manuscript, which stunned me. By then, one kid had started school, granting me larger chunks of time, and I thought maybe, *maybe*, I could somehow weave these into a book of sorts. Now my kids are eight and eleven, and after years of consistent writing in ten-minute or two-hour chunks of time, my first book—built on the foundation of these shorts—is forthcoming.

I could tell you more inspiring things, like the way I scribble words and phrases on hotel notepads every day, recording anything that catches my creative attention. I could tell you how I transcribe these notes onto note cards and keep them in a recipe box on my desk so that I might later pull out a card that reads, *Dick Cheney, bunker, divorce, contact dermatitis*, and how I then craft an essay from these disparate elements, letting them collide and spark. And I could say that watching the larger story emerge from these details as I write is the real magic, the *why* of my writing (because it is).

But that might eclipse the biggest lesson of my domestic, post-MFA life, which is that endurance and sustained attention are everything. In the end, it doesn't matter when or how the work got done. It matters that it *did* get done, one tiny piece at a time.

Writing Prompts

As in previous parts, these prompts consider starting points in image and story, focusing here in particular on moments of transition for children and mothers. Several prompts also draw from the more experimental poems and look at their structures as scaffolds that might support new possibilities. As you write, consider using Melissa Stephenson's technique of index cards or Emari DiGiorgio's audio drafting strategy.

1) In "More Moon" by Kim-An Lieberman, both the child and the mother look at a single image, the moon, and have different thoughts about it. The moon, in its waxing and waning, becomes a symbol for the cycle of life and death. What is something that you and your child see differently? How can that object function as a symbol? Bring that object and both perspectives into the poem.
2) Mahogany L. Browne in "Inevitable" picks an event that feels like a coming-of-age moment in the life of her child, her daughter's first homecoming dance. The speaker in this poem suddenly sees her daughter in a new light and uses anaphora (the repetition of the phrase "I tried not") to create some momentum in the description. Pick a turning-point moment in your own or your child's life to write about, starting in what is real and imagining the future that follows.
   a) Incorporate anaphora, repeating a specific phrase at the start of each sentence or line to create rhythm.
   b) By trying "not to," Browne indicates what she did, in fact, *do*, creating conflict within herself. Use Browne's phrase, or another like it, to create tension in the poem.

3) In “Two Glasses of Milk” Teri Ellen Cross Davis uses images (the perfectly folded napkin, the glasses of milk) and allusion (the reference to Sylvia Plath’s suicide) to show how a mother may attempt to provide for everyone, to see to every last detail, even when on the brink of her own self-destruction. This creates a startling juxtaposition. Cross Davis weaves into the poem her own experience, the weight she is carrying as a mother, poet, and wife.
   a) Pick a story you know—from fiction, history, or the news—in which a mother does something startling. As you imagine the scene into a poem, include specific details that show the mother still “tending to” her role as mother.
   b) Like Sarah Vap, write your child’s interruptions into the poem. Let the words or events, as unpoetic as they may be, appear when they appear, and let them shift your direction and thought process.
4) Many of the writers in this collection work full-time outside the home while raising children. While several work in academia, others work in jobs ranging from web designer, to freelance writer, to editor. No matter where they work, writer-mothers must balance the demands of work and parenting alongside the demands of writing. Write a poem about work in which parenting intrudes, or write a poem about parenting in which work intrudes. Or, taking a cue from Melissa Stephenson’s “Confetti Time,” write a brief essay that acknowledges the demands on your time and then gives you both the strategies and encouragement you need to keep writing.
5) In “Our Family on the Run,” Brenda Shaughnessy imagines her family in an apocalyptic scene as the basis for a poem full of lists and action. Imagine your family in a high-pressure circumstance—one where time is essential. It need not be a disaster—even getting out the door can feel high-pressure—and focus on the unfolding event and how the family works (or does not work) together.
6) Vanessa Angélica Villarreal uses another form she knows, computer coding, in “*ƒ*= [*(root) (future)*].” Because the code moves horizontally and vertically, allowing for the left and right sides to occur simultaneously, Villarreal is able to open up new possibilities for how time passes through familial generations. Pick a form not traditionally associated with poetry—a Venn diagram, a recipe, a packing list, a blueprint—and use the format to open new possibilities for your poem’s content.

Afterword

On the eve of a historic election, it is hard to think of anything else but this moment of precipice that we sit on as a nation that is fractured and uncertain. Regardless of the political outcome, the numbers game, the country faces a reckoning that's been long overdue. That political urgency informs how I'm refracting the experience of revisiting this book that I've known in many iterations. The topic of motherhood is at stake in the outcome of the election, relevant for example when Lindsey Graham suggests that young women can succeed if they follow a "traditional family structure." This book is a resistance to Graham's notion. Motherhood is no binary: all lives are bound to the biological terms of maternity. This collection draws from epistemological and embodied threads. Many of the anthology's poets speak to the perceptive acuity wrought from being a mother, like Carrie Fountain's ode "To White Noise." Diannely Antigua toys with the question of "the mother in me" at a taco place. Jordan Rice writes about "the extent to which having a child revises the illusion of self" in the essay "If I Admit Who I Am, Who Will I Become?," which describes her journey with her transgendered legibility as a parent, though the theme of motherhood's revision recurs.

In many of these works, the writers' implicit question is about the liminal space between mother and artist and the pull of both forces.

The writers in these pages I'm honored to be part of are woken up or go to sleep sleepless with anxiety and sometimes wonder. They mourn in mythologies and contend with being adjacent purely to source and center. Motherhood's import is all our legacies, after all. I'm dazzled by the scale of this book's expansive vision of being mother and of doing mother. I was happy to be challenged and invited to write at the book's end. I had lost my way to a lot of the questions I still had to contend with as a mother of teenaged children. Whatever sense of expertise I felt has gone out of the window, and reading this book reminded me of the fantastic coven of fellow travelers that offer solace and wisdom in their writerly-motherly subjectivities. Lisa L. Moore's "Sunday Dinner" is an essay I'll continue to refer to as a lesbian mom raising cisgender kids myself. She writes, "so that I may repay my debt to the world, I acknowledge joy." This book ultimately renders visible the terrific sublimity of art's cathartic and inquiring possibility. We can't be bewildered without art.

Women are always at the forefront of revolutions and so are artists. I'm so grateful for the visionary curatorial work of Emily Pérez and Nancy Reddy for gathering us for the occasion of this book and to the writers who so generously delved into the bewilderments of motherhood as paradigm.

CARMEN GIMÉNEZ SMITH
November 2, 2020

Acknowledgments

This book began as a panel, "Writing/Motherhood: Difficulty, Ambivalence, and Joy," at the Association of Writers and Writing Programs conference in Tampa in the spring of 2018. We were scheduled for 9:00 a.m. on the very first day of the conference. Still, the large room was full of writers and writer/mothers eager to talk. For the rest of the weekend, writers stopped us in the book fair and hallways of the convention center to say how much they'd liked the panel and to explain how much they'd needed the conversation and affirmation of other writers working through writing and mothering. We were convinced that there was more work to be done—more perspectives on motherhood, more ways of thinking about writing/motherhood—and we decided we wanted to make a book.

We quickly realized we didn't actually know how to create an anthology, and we're grateful to the writers who lent their expertise early in this project, especially Camille T. Dungy, Sarah Green, Stephanie G'Schwind, Jesse Lee Kercheval, and Shara Lessley. As the project has progressed, Camille T. Dungy's encouragement and practical support have been essential, as has her example of a poet writing motherhood. Thanks to Carmen Giménez Smith, whose *Bring Down the Little Birds* inspired us both, and who in the very early days said, "I would do ANYTHING to support this book." Special thanks to Carolina Ebeid, Chanda Feldman, and Chelsea Rathburn, who have been with us from that very first early morning panel.

We're grateful to the Sustainable Arts Foundation and Tony and Caroline Grant for financial support for this project and for their commitment to supporting and celebrating parents who are artists.

Thanks to the staff of the University of Georgia Press, especially our acquisitions editor, Beth Snead, for enthusiasm for our vision and for shepherding this book from proposal to publication. Thanks to the copyediting team, Madison Esters, Megan N. Fontenot, and Thomas Roche, for their care and attention.

We'd also like to thank the teachers, therapists, and childcare providers whose care for our children made this work possible. Emily would like to thank her parents, K. C. Atha, Carla Gorrell, Liza Skipwith, Kate O'Donnell, and Park Hill Elementary, all of whom have played roles—direct and indirect—in supporting her children. Nancy would like to thank the staff at Haddon Learning Center, the teachers and administrators at Thomas Sharp Elementary and James A. Garfield Elementary, and the staff of the Just Kids aftercare program.

I, Nancy, would like to thank my family, including my husband Smith and my sons Penn and Finn. Love and admiration for my mother, Marilyn Seigh. Because I grew up with a working mother, because I saw work as normal and important and compatible with family life, I never doubted that I would pursue a career and have children. I'll always be grateful to have had that example. I'm thankful for the support of my colleagues in the writing program at Stockton University, and particularly for the example of writing/motherhood offered by Emily Van Duyne and Emari DiGiorgio. Thanks especially to Emari, who insisted at crucial moments that it's important for children to see their mothers working hard at projects that matter, even if it means being away from home.

To Emily Pérez, thank you for your eagerness in taking on this project with me, and for your steadfast partnership as it became bigger and more time-consuming and more exciting than either of us originally imagined. I'm grateful for your keen editorial eye (even though it cost me many beloved modifiers!) and for the wide reading that brought so many wonderful poets into this collection.

I, Emily, want to thank Julie Irons, Jenn Kao, and Jenny Tran, whose ideas were crucial in the early stages of this book. Thanks go to my sister, Ileana Street, who lent both moral support and her business prowess as we pulled together our proposal. Thanks to my parents who taught me to pursue my dreams. Thanks to so many poets in this book whose ideas about other poets and poems to pursue led to a wealth of voices. To Nina McConigley, Jill Meyers, Amanda Nowlin-O'Banion, Mónica Parle, Sasha West, and Tiphanie Yanique for modeling many ways to be mother-writers. To Cari Treviño, always. Love and gratitude to my own family, who made me a mother. Wylan and Felix, you are the greatest gift. Matt, your love, encouragement, and parenting hours have made this work possible.

To Nancy Reddy, what began as a great working relationship has flourished into a friendship. I admire your organization and perseverance, your strategic sense, and your hustle. I have learned so much from you.

About the Contributors

Editors

EMILY PÉREZ is the author of *What Flies Want*, winner of the Iowa Poetry Prize (University of Iowa Press, 2022); *House of Sugar, House of Stone* (Center for Literary Publishing, 2016); and the chapbooks *Made and Unmade* (Madhouse Press, 2019) and *Backyard Migration Route* (Finishing Line Press, 2011). She graduated with honors from Stanford University and earned an MFA at the University of Houston, where she served as a poetry editor for *Gulf Coast* and taught with Writers in the Schools. A CantoMundo fellow and Ledbury Emerging Critic, she has received funding and support from the Washington State Artist Trust, Jack Straw Writers, Bread Loaf Writers' Workshop, Summer Literary Seminars, and the Community of Writers. Her poems have appeared in journals including *Copper Nickel*, *Fairy Tale Review*, *Prairie Schooner*, and *Poetry*. Her work as a reviewer has appeared in *RHINO*, the *Rumpus*, the *Guardian*, and elsewhere. She teaches English and gender studies in Denver, where she lives with her family.

NANCY REDDY is the author of *Pocket Universe* (Louisiana State University Press, 2022); *Double Jinx* (Milkweed Editions, 2015), a 2014 winner of the National Poetry Series; and *Acadiana* (Black Lawrence Press, 2018). She holds a PhD in composition and rhetoric and an MFA in poetry from the University of Wisconsin, Madison. Her poems have appeared or are forthcoming in *Pleiades*, *Blackbird*, *Colorado Review*, the *Iowa Review*, the *Gettysburg Review*, *Smartish Pace*, and elsewhere. She is the recipient of grants from the Sustainable Arts Foundation and the New Jersey State Council on the Arts, and she was awarded a Walter E. Dakin Fellowship from the Sewanee Writers' Conference. She teaches in the writing First Year Studies programs at Stockton University and lives outside Philadelphia with her family.

Authors

DIANNELY ANTIGUA is a Dominican American poet and educator. Her debut collection *Ugly Music* was the winner of the Pamet River Prize and a Whiting Award. She is the recipient of fellowships from CantoMundo, Community of Writers, and the Fine Arts Work Center Summer Program. Her work has been nominated for both the Pushcart Prize and Best of the Net.

ZEINA HASHEM BECK is a Lebanese poet. Her newest poetry collection is *O*. She is also the author of *Louder than Hearts, To Live in Autumn, 3arabi Song*, and *There Was and How Much There Was*.

REMICA BINGHAM-RISHER, a native of Phoenix, Arizona, is a Cave Canem fellow and Affrilachian Poet. She is the author of *Conversion, What We Ask of Flesh*, and *Starlight & Error*, winner of the Diode Editions Book Award. She is the director of Quality Enhancement Plan Initiatives at Old Dominion University in Norfolk, Virginia, where she resides with her husband and children.

SARAH BLAKE is the author of two novels, *Clean Air* and *Naamah*, two books of poetry, *Let's Not Live on Earth* and *Mr. West*, and one chapbook, *Named after Death*. A past NEA fellow, Blake now lives in the United Kingdom.

ALLISON BLEVINS is the author of *Slowly/Suddenly* and the chapbooks *Susurration, Letters to Joan, A Season for Speaking*, and *Chorus for the Kill*. She is the director of Small Harbor Publishing and the executive editor at *the museum of americana*. She lives in Missouri with her spouse and three children.

MAHOGANY L. BROWNE is coeditor of *The BreakBeat Poets Volume 2: Black Girl Magic* and author of *Black Girl Magic* and *Redbone*.

JULIE CARR is the author of six books of poetry, including *100 Notes on Violence, RAG*, and *Think Tank*, and of several prose works. Carr is a professor at the University of Colorado in Boulder. With Tim Roberts she is the cofounder of Counterpath Press, Counterpath Gallery, and Counterpath Community Garden in Denver.

SUNU P. CHANDY is the daughter of immigrants. She is also a parent, poet, social justice activist, and civil rights attorney. Sunu's publications can be found in *Beltway Poetry Quarterly, Asian American Literary Review*, and *This Bridge We Call Home: Radical Visions for Transformation*. She is currently the legal director at the National Women's Law Center.

TINA CHANG is an American poet, teacher, and editor. In 2010, she was the first woman to be named poet laureate of Brooklyn. She is the author of three poetry collections: *Hybrida, Of Gods & Strangers*, and *Half-Lit Houses*. Tina Chang received her MFA in poetry from Columbia University. She is a professor and director of creative writing at Binghamton University.

VICTORIA CHANG's poetry books include *OBIT, Barbie Chang, The Boss, Salvinia Molesta*, and *Circle*. *OBIT* received the Anisfield-Wolf Book Award, the *Los*

Angeles Times Book Prize, and the PEN Voelcker Award. Recipient of a Guggenheim Fellowship and many other awards, she lives in Los Angeles.

NICOLE COOLEY's most recent books are two poetry collections, *Girl after Girl after Girl* and *Of Marriage*. Her awards include the Walt Whitman Award from the Academy of American Poets, a Discovery/The Nation Award, an NEA fellowship, and others. She is the director of the MFA Program at Queens College, City University of New York.

TERI ELLEN CROSS DAVIS is the author of *a more perfect Union*, winner of *The Journal*/Charles B. Wheeler Poetry Prize, and *Haint*, winner of the Ohioana Book Award. A Cave Canem fellow and the poetry coordinator for the Folger Shakespeare Library, she lives in Maryland with her husband, the poet Hayes Davis, and their two children.

LAURA DA' is the author of *Instruments of the True Measure* and *Tributaries*, which received an American Book Award from the Before Columbus Foundation. She is the recipient of fellowships from Hugo House and the Jack Straw Writers Program. Da', who is Eastern Shawnee, lives near Seattle, Washington.

MEG DAY is the author of *Last Psalm at Sea Level*, winner of the Publishing Triangle's Audre Lorde Award and a finalist for the Kate Tufts Discovery Award, and the coeditor of *Laura Hershey: On the Life & Work of an American Master*. An NEA fellowship winner, Day is assistant professor of English & creative writing at Franklin & Marshall College.

KENDRA DECOLO is the author of *I Am Not Trying to Hide My Hungers from the World*, *My Dinner with Ron Jeremy*, and *Thieves in the Afterlife*. She has received awards and fellowships from the NEA, MacDowell, the Bread Loaf Writers' Conference, and others. She teaches at Hugo House, and she lives in Nashville, Tennessee.

EMARI DIGIORGIO is the author of *Girl Torpedo*, winner of the Numinous Orison, Luminous Origin Literary Award, and *The Things a Body Might Become*. She teaches at Stockton University, is a Geraldine R. Dodge Foundation Poet, and hosts World Above, a monthly reading series in Atlantic City, New Jersey.

CHELSEA DINGMAN's first book, *Thaw*, was chosen by Allison Joseph as winner of the National Poetry Series. Her second poetry collection, *Through a Small Ghost*, won the Georgia Poetry Prize. She is also the author of the chapbook *What Bodies Have I Moved*.

ALEXA DORAN is the author of *DM Me, Mother Darling* and the chapbook *Nightsink, Faucet Me a Lullaby*. She earned a PhD in poetry at Florida State University. Her series of poems about the women of Dada, "The Octopus Breath on Her Neck," was recently released as part of Oxidant/Engine's *BoxSet* series, vol. 2.

CAMILLE T. DUNGY's debut collection of personal essays is *Guidebook to Relative Strangers*, a finalist for the National Book Critics Circle Award. She is also the author of four collections of poetry, most recently *Trophic Cas-*

cade, winner of the Colorado Book Award. Honors include fellowships from the Guggenheim Foundation and the NEA.

CAROLINA EBEID is the author of *You Ask Me to Talk about the Interior*. She holds a PhD from the University of Denver and has won fellowships from the Stadler Center, the NEA, and the Lannan Foundation Residency. She edits poetry at *The Rumpus* as well as helps to create the online zine *Visible Binary* together with her husband and son.

HEID E. ERDRICH is the author of *Little Big Bully* and editor of the anthology *New Poets of Native Nations*. She has won awards for her writing from the National Poetry Series, Native Arts and Cultures Foundation, and Loft Literary Center, among others. Heid grew up in Wahpeton, North Dakota, and is Ojibwe enrolled at Turtle Mountain.

CHANDA FELDMAN is the author of *Approaching the Fields*. She has received awards and fellowships from the Bread Loaf Writers' Conference, the Cave Canem Foundation, the MacDowell Colony, and the NEA, and she was a Wallace Stegner Fellow at Stanford University. Chanda is an assistant professor of creative writing at Oberlin College.

BETH ANN FENNELLY, poet laureate of Mississippi, teaches in the MFA Program at the University of Mississippi. She has won grants and awards from the NEA, the United States Artists, and others. Author of three poetry books, *Open House*, *Tender Hooks*, and *Unmentionables*, and three books of prose, Fennelly lives with her husband and three children in Oxford.

CARRIE FOUNTAIN is the author of the poetry collections *Burn Lake*, a National Poetry Series winner; *Instant Winner*; and *The Life*. *I'm Not Missing* is her debut novel for young adults, and her first children's book, *The Poem Forest*, about the life and legacy of poet and ecologist W. S. Merwin, is forthcoming.

KRISTA FRANKLIN is a writer and visual artist, the author of *Too Much Midnight*, the artist book *Under the Knife*, and the chapbook *Study of Love & Black Body*. She is a Helen and Tim Meier Foundation for the Arts Achievement Awardee and a recipient of the Joan Mitchell Foundation Painters and Sculptors Grant.

SHAMALA GALLAGHER is a queer, mixed-race, bipolar poet and essayist and the mother of a toddler. She is the author of *Late Morning Where the World Burns*. A Kundiman fellow, she holds an MFA from the Michener Center for Writers and a PhD from the University of Georgia. She writes, edits, teaches, and parents in Athens, Georgia.

SHERINE GILMOUR graduated with an MFA in poetry from New York University. She has been nominated for a Pushcart Prize, and her poems have appeared in or are forthcoming from *Glass: A Journal of Poetry*, the *Indianapolis Review*, *River Styx*, *So To Speak*, *Tinderbox*, and other publications.

CARMEN GIMÉNEZ SMITH, a Guggenheim fellow, is the author of seven books, including *Milk and Filth*, a finalist for the National Book Critics Circle Award in poetry, and *Be Recorder*, a finalist for the National Book Award and the PEN Open Book Award. She is publisher of Noemi Press and a professor of English at Virginia Tech.

ARACELIS GIRMAY is the author of three collections of poetry: *the black maria*, *Kingdom Animalia*, and *Teeth*. She curated *How to Carry Water: Selected Poems of Lucille Clifton*. Girmay is on the editorial board of the African Poetry Book Fund.

JENN GIVHAN is a Mexican American poet who has received NEA and PEN/Rosenthal Emerging Voices fellowships. She has been published in the *New Republic*, *Salon*, and *Poetry*. The author of four collections of poetry and the novels *Trinity Sight* and *Jubilee*, she lives with her family in New Mexico.

CAMILLE GUTHRIE is the author of four books of poetry: *Diamonds*, *Articulated Lair: Poems for Louise Bourgeois*, *In Captivity*, and *The Master Thief*. The director of the Undergraduate Writing Initiatives at Bennington College, she has been awarded fellowships from MacDowell and Yaddo. Currently, she lives in rural Vermont with her two children.

LAUREN HALDEMAN is the author of the books *Instead of Dying*, winner of the Colorado Prize for Poetry, and *Calenday*. A graphic novelist and poet, she is a recipient of fellowships and awards from the Iowa Arts Council, the Sustainable Arts Foundation, and the Iowa Writers' Workshop.

PAMELA HART is the writer in residence at the Katonah Museum of Art. Her book *Mothers over Nangarhar* won the Kathryn A. Morton prize. An NEA fellowship recipient, she is an editor for Afghan Voices, the Afghan Women's Writing Project, and *As You Were: The Military Review*. Her poems have been published in various online and print journals.

FAYLITA HICKS (she/they) is a writer and justice impacted organizer specializing in pretrial justice reform in rural communities and the cultural impact of trauma on queer Black people. They are the author of *HoodWitch* and Civil Rights Corps' Poet-in-Residence. Hicks was awarded fellowships from Lambda Literary and Jack Jones Literary Arts.

JOAN NAVIYUK KANE is the author of eight collections of poetry and prose whose most recent book is *Dark Traffic*. She was the 2021 Mary Routt Chair of Creative Writing and Journalism at Scripps College and has received a Whiting Award, the Donald Hall Prize, an American Book Award, and a Guggenheim Fellowship. She raises her sons as a single mother in Cambridge, Massachusetts.

JOY KATZ writes about whiteness, tennis, adoption, and other things. Her most recent poetry collection is *All You Do Is Perceive*. A past NEA and Stegner fellow, she teaches off the tenure track in MFA programs around the country and in Carlow University's long-running Madwomen in the Attic workshops for women. She also collaborates in the Pittsburgh-based activist art collective IfYouReallyLoveMe.

KEETJE KUIPERS is the author of three books of poems: *Beautiful in the Mouth*, *The Keys to the Jail*, and, most recently, *All Its Charms*. Keetje has been a Stegner Fellow, a Bread Loaf fellow, and PEN Northwest's Margery Davis Boyden Wilderness Writing Resident. She lives with her wife and children on an island in the Salish Sea. She is editor of *Poetry Northwest.*

JOY LADIN is the author of nine books of poetry, most recently *The Future Is Trying to Tell Us Something: New and Selected Poems.* A new edition of her second book, *The Book of Anna*, has just been published by EOAGH Press. A nationally recognized speaker on gender and Jewish identity, she has been featured on NPR's "On Being with Krista Tippett."

EUGENIA LEIGH is a Korean American poet and the author of two collections of poetry, *Bianca and Blood* and *Sparrows and Sparrows*. The recipient of fellowships and awards from *Poets & Writers Magazine*, Kundiman, *Rattle*, the Frost Place, and elsewhere, Eugenia received her MFA from Sarah Lawrence College.

RAINA J. LEÓN is a fellow of Cave Canem, CantoMundo, Macondo, and Obsidian Foundation (UK), and a member of the Carolina African American Writers Collective. Her collections of poetry include *Canticle of Idols*, *Boogeyman Dawn*, and *sombra : (dis)locate*. She is a founding editor of the *Acentos Review*, an online quarterly devoted to the promotion and publication of Latinx arts, and cofounder of StoryJoy, Inc.

SHARA LESSLEY is the author of *The Explosive Expert's Wife* and *Two-Headed Nightingale* and coeditor of *The Poem's Country: Place & Poetic Practice*, an anthology of essays. A former Stegner Fellow at Stanford, she has won an NEA fellowship and other awards. Consulting editor for Acre Books, she currently lives in Dubai.

KIM-AN LIEBERMAN was a writer of Vietnamese and Jewish American descent. The author of *Breaking the Map* and *In Orbit*, she received awards from Jack Straw Writers and the Mellon Foundation, and she spent many years teaching literature and writing. Kim-An was diagnosed with late-stage gastric cancer in 2011 at the age of thirty-seven. She died in 2013.

LAYLI LONG SOLDIER is the author of *Whereas*, which won the PEN/Jean Stein Book Award and was short-listed for the National Book Award. Long Soldier has received a Lannan Literary Fellowship, a National Artist Fellowship from the Native Arts and Cultures Foundation, and a Whiting Award. She lives in Santa Fe, New Mexico.

KWOYA FAGIN MAPLES is a writer from Charleston, South Carolina. She holds an MFA in creative writing from the University of Alabama and is a Cave Canem Fellow and a current Alabama State Council on the Arts Literary Fellow. She is the author of *Mend*, which was named a 2019 Finalist for the Hurston/Wright Legacy Award for Poetry.

JOYELLE MCSWEENEY is the author of ten books, most recently *Toxicon & Arachne*, *The Necropastoral: Poetry, Media, Occults*, and *Dead Youth; or, The Leaks*, a verse play that inaugurated the Leslie Scalapino Prize for Innovative Women Performance Writers. She coedits Action Books and teaches at the University of Notre Dame.

ERIKA MEITNER is the author of six books of poems, including *Ideal Cities*, a National Poetry Series winner; *Copia*; and *Holy Moly Carry Me*, winner of the 2018 National Jewish Book Award in poetry and a finalist for the National Book Critics Circle Award. Her most recent collection is *Useful Junk*. Meitner is currently a professor of English at Virginia Tech.

LYNN MELNICK is the author of the poetry collections *Refusenik*, *Landscape with Sex and Violence*, and *If I Should Say I Have Hope*. *I've Had to Think Up a Way to Survive*, a book about Dolly Parton that is also a bit of a memoir, is forthcoming from University of Texas Press.

JASMINNE MENDEZ is a Dominican American poet, playwright, and podcast host. She is the author of *Machete*, *Island of Dreams*, and *Night-Blooming Jasmin(n)e: Personal Essays and Poetry*. She is a CantoMundo Fellow and a graduate of the creative writing program at the Rainier Writing Workshop at Pacific Lutheran University.

CLARISSA MENDIOLA is a native daughter of Guåhan (Guam). As a Chamoru woman raised in diaspora, she writes poetry to bridge the distance between her home island and where she stands. A former Hedgebrook Writer in Residence, she currently teaches creative writing camps at a San Francisco high school, where she also serves as a communications writer.

EMILY MOHN-SLATE is the author of *The Falls*, winner of the New American Poetry Prize, and *Feed*, winner of the Keystone Chapbook Prize. She lives in Pittsburgh, Pennsylvania, where she teaches high school English by day and poetry workshops for the Madwomen in the Attic at Carlow University by night.

LISA L. MOORE is the author of *Sister Arts: The Erotics of Lesbian Landscapes* (Lambda Literary Award) and the poetry collection *24 Hours of Men*. She is Archibald A. Hill Professor of English, professor of women's and gender studies, and director of the program in LGBTQ Studies at the University of Texas at Austin.

SARA MUMOLO is the author of *Day Counter* and *Mortar*. She serves as the associate director for the MFA in creative writing at Saint Mary's College of California. She has received residencies to Vermont Studio Center and Caldera Center for the Arts, and she was named a spring 2021 Poetry and the Senses fellow for the Arts and Research Center at UC Berkeley.

AIMEE NEZHUKUMATATHIL is the author of the *New York Times* best-selling *World of Wonders: In Praise of Fireflies, Whale Sharks, & Other Astonishments* and four poetry collections. Honors include fellowships from the NEA and Guggenheim Foundation and a Mississippi Arts Council grant. She is professor in the University of Mississippi's MFA program.

JANUARY GILL O'NEIL is the author of *Rewilding*, *Misery Islands*, and *Underlife*. She is an associate professor of English at Salem State University and board member with the Association of Writers and Writing Programs (AWP), Mass Poetry, and Montserrat College of Art. She lives with her two children in Beverly, Massachusetts.

EMMY PÉREZ, Texas poet laureate in 2020, is the author of the poetry collections *With the River on Our Face* and *Solstice*. A volume of her new and selected works is forthcoming. A recipient of poetry fellowships from the Academy of American Poets, the NEA, and others, she is professor of creative writing at the University of Texas, Rio Grande Valley.

KIKI PETROSINO is the author of four books of poetry: *White Blood: a Lyric of Virginia*, *Witch Wife*, *Hymn for the Black Terrific*, and *Fort Red Border*. She teaches at the University of Virginia as a professor of poetry. Petrosino is the recipient of a Pushcart Prize, a Fellowship in Creative Writing from the NEA, and an Al Smith Fellowship Award from the Kentucky Arts Council.

CATHERINE PIERCE is the author of four books of poems, including *Danger Days*. Her work has appeared in *The Best American Poetry*, the Academy of American Poets' Poem-a-Day series, and elsewhere. An NEA Fellow and two-time Pushcart Prize winner, she codirects the creative writing program at Mississippi State University.

KHADIJAH QUEEN is the author of six books, most recently *Anodyne* and *I'm So Fine: A List of Famous Men & What I Had On*. Her verse play *Non-Sequitur* won the Leslie Scalapino Award for Innovative Women's Performance Writing. She is an associate professor of creative writing at Virginia Tech and holds a PhD in English from the University of Denver.

CHELSEA RATHBURN is the author of three full-length poetry collections, most recently *Still Life with Mother and Knife*, a *New York Times* "New & Noteworthy" book. Recipient of a 2009 NEA poetry fellowship, Rathburn was appointed poet laureate of Georgia in 2019.

JORDAN RICE is the author of *Constellarium*, a finalist for the 2017 Kate Tufts Award. She lives in Richmond, Virginia.

NATALIE SHAPERO is the author, most recently, of the poetry collection *Popular Longing*. She is the recipient of an NEA Fellowship, a Ruth Lilly Fellowship, and a *Kenyon Review* Fellowship. She is professor of the practice of poetry at Tufts University, and she has previously worked as a civil rights lawyer and as a literary editor.

BRENDA SHAUGHNESSY is the author of five poetry collections, including *The Octopus Museum*, *So Much Synth*, and *Our Andromeda*, which was a finalist for the Kingsley Tufts Award, the International Griffin Prize, and the PEN Open Book Award. A Guggenheim Fellow, she is professor of English and creative writing at Rutgers University, Newark.

신선영 SUN YUNG SHIN is the author of poetry collections *The Wet Hex*; *Unbearable Splendor*; *Rough, and Savage*; and *Skirt Full of Black*. She is the editor of *What We Hunger For: Refugees & Immigrants on Food & Family*, and *A Good Time for the Truth: Race in Minnesota*, and she is coeditor of *Outsiders Within: Writing on Transracial Adoption*.

MAGGIE SMITH is the author of five books, most recently *Goldenrod*, *Good Bones*, and *Keep Moving: Notes on Loss, Creativity, and Change*. A freelance writer and editor, Smith is on the poetry faculty of Spalding University's MFA program and serves as an editor at large for the *Kenyon Review*.

MEGAN SNYDER-CAMP is the author of three books of poetry: *The Forest of Sure Things*, *Wintering*, and *The Gunnywolf*. She has received grants and fellowships from the Bread Loaf Writers' Conference, Djerassi, the 4Culture Foundation, and the Richard Hugo House. She lives in Seattle.

MOLLY SPENCER's debut poetry collection, *If the House*, won the 2019 Brittingham Prize judged by Carl Phillips. A second collection, *Hinge*, won the 2019 Crab Orchard Open Competition judged by Allison Joseph. She is a senior poetry editor at the *Rumpus* and teaches at the University of Michigan's Gerald R. Ford School of Public Policy.

MELISSA STEPHENSON's writing has appeared in publications such as the *Rumpus*, the *Washington Post*, *Ms. Magazine*, *ZYZZYVA*, *LitHub*, and *Fourth Genre*. Her memoir, *Driven*, was released by Houghton Mifflin Harcourt. She lives in Missoula, Montana, with her two kids.

ALISON STINE is the author of the novels *Road Out of Winter* and *Trashlands* and three poetry collections, most recently *Wait*, winner of the Brittingham Prize. She has been a recipient of an Individual Artist Fellowship from the NEA, an Ohio Arts Council grant, and a reporting grant from *National Geographic*, and she was a Wallace Stegner Fellow.

ANGELA NARCISO TORRES is the author of *What Happens Is Neither*, *Blood Orange*, winner of the 2013 Willow Books Literature Award, and the chapbook *To the Bone*. A graduate of Warren Wilson MFA Program and Harvard Graduate School of Education, Angela has received fellowships from Bread Loaf Writers' Conference, Illinois Arts Council, and Ragdale Foundation.

LENA KHALAF TUFFAHA is a poet, essayist, and translator. Her first full-length collection of poems, *Water & Salt*, won the Washington State Book Award for Poetry. She is also the author of two chapbooks, *Arab in Newsland*, selected by poet January Gill O'Neil for the Two Sylvias Prize, and *Letters from the Interior*.

SARAH VAP is an American writer and the author of seven books of poetry, poetics, and nonfiction, most recently *Winter: Effulgences and Devotions*. Her collection *Viability* was selected for the National Poetry Series; her book *American Spikenard* was awarded the Iowa Poetry Prize. She taught in the MFA program at Drew University.

VANESSA ANGÉLICA VILLARREAL is the author of the collection *Beast Meridian*, a 2019 Whiting Award recipient, a Kate Tufts Discovery Award finalist, and winner of the John A. Robertson Award for the Best First Book of Poetry from the Texas Institute of Letters. She is a recipient of a 2021 NEA Poetry Fellowship and fellowships from CantoMundo and Jack Jones Literary Arts.

HOPE WABUKE is a poet, writer, and assistant professor at the University of Nebraska, Lincoln. She is the author of the poetry collection *The Body Family* and the memoir *Please Don't Kill My Black Son, Please*. Hope has received fellowships and awards from the NEA, the National Book Critics Circle, the *New York Times* Foundation, Cave Canem, and the Poetry Foundation.

SASHA WEST's first book, *Failure and I Bury the Body*, was a winner of the National Poetry Series, the Texas Institute of Letters First Book of Poetry Award, and a Bread Loaf Writers' Conference Fellowship. She is an associate professor of creative writing at St. Edward's University in Austin, Texas.

MONICA YOUN is the author of *Blackacre*, which won the William Carlos Williams Award, was a finalist for the National Book Critic Circle Award and the Kingsley Tufts Award, and was longlisted for the National Book Award. Her previous poetry collections are *Ignatz*, which was a finalist for the National Book Award, and *Barter*. A Guggenheim Fellow, she is the daughter of Korean immigrants.

RACHEL ZUCKER is the author of ten books, including *SoundMachine*, the memoir *MOTHERs*, and *Museum of Accidents*, which was a finalist for the National Book Critics Circle Award. A recipient of fellowships from the NEA and MacDowell, Zucker is the founder and host of the podcast *Commonplace: Conversations with Poets (and Other People)*.

Credits

Diannely Antigua, "Re-Education," in *Ugly Music* (YesYes Books, 2019).
Zeina Hashem Beck, "Ode to Disappointment," in *TriQuarterly*.
Remica Bingham-Risher, "We See *The Lion King* on Broadway, I Enter the Pride," in *Starlight & Error* (Diode Editions, 2017).
"Suicide Prevention" from *Let's Not Live on Earth* © 2018 by Sarah Blake. Published by Wesleyan University Press. Reprinted with permission.
Allison Blevins, "My Daughter Returns from My Ex-Wife's House with Braids in Her Hair," *Susurration* (Blue Lyra Press, 2019); also published in *Hashtag Queer: LGBTQ+ Creative Anthology Volume #2*, ed. Sage Kalmus (Qommunity LLC, 2018).
Mahogany L. Browne, "Inevitable," in Academy of American Poets Poem-a-Day. © 2019 by Mahogany L. Browne.
Julie Carr, "A Short Prose Piece on One of the Book's Central Themes," in *Real Life: An Installation* (Omnidawn, 2018).
Sunu P. Chandy, "Kasthaputta Vanhu," in *Beltway Poetry Quarterly*. Reprinted with permission of the author.
"Revolutionary Kiss," from *Hybrida: Poems* by Tina Chang. Copyright © 2019 by Tina Chang. Used by permission of W. W. Norton & Company, Inc.
Victoria Chang, "Dear P.," from *Barbie Chang*. Copyright © 2017 by Victoria Chang. Reprinted with the permission of The Permissions Company, LLC on behalf of Copper Canyon Press, www.coppercanyonpress.org.
Nicole Cooley, "Homeland Security," from *Milk Dress*. Copyright © 2010 by Nicole Cooley. Reprinted with the permission of The Permissions Company, LLC on behalf of Alice James Books, www.alicejamesbooks.org.
"Two Glasses of Milk" from "Haint." Copyright © Teri Ellen Cross Davis. Reprinted by permission of Gival Press.
"Earth Mover" from *Tributaries* by Laura Da' © 2015 Laura Da'. Reprinted by permission of the University of Arizona Press.
Meg Day, "To My Brother, in Her Barrenness," in *The Rumpus*.
Kendra DeColo, "I Pump Milk like a Boss," from *I Am Not Trying to Hide My Hungers from the World*. Originally in *Los Angeles Review*. Copyright © 2020, 2021 by Kendra

DeColo. Reprinted with the permission of The Permissions Company, LLC on behalf of BOA Editions, Ltd., boaeditions.org.

Emari DiGiorgio, "Fallible Beasts," in *Girl Torpedo* (Agape Editions, 2018).

Chelsea Dingman, "Self Portrait as God with a Stillborn Inside." Publication first appeared in *Radar Poetry*. From *Through a Small Ghost* by Chelsea Dingman. Copyright 2020 by Chelsea Dingman. Used by permission of the University of Georgia Press.

Alexa Doran, "C-Section," in *Nightsink, Faucet Me a Lullaby* (Bottlecap Press, 2019).

Camille T. Dungy, "The Average Mother Now Spends Twice as Many Hours on Childcare as Did Her Counterpart in 1965, and She Also Spends Three Times as Many Hours Working Outside the Home; or, How to Sing a Song of Sixpence When You're Really Feeling Wry," in *The Paris Review*.

Carolina Ebeid, "Veronicas of a Matador," in *You Ask Me to Talk about the Interior* (Noemi Press, 2016).

Heid E. Erdrich, "Intimate Detail," in *The Mother's Tongue* (Salt Publishing, 2006). Reproduced with permission of Salt Publishing through PLSclear.

Chanda Feldman, "Laboring," in *Approaching the Fields* (Louisiana State University Press, 2018).

"Latching On, Falling Off," from *Tender Hooks: Poems* by Beth Ann Fennelly. Copyright © 2004 by Beth Ann Fennelly. Used by permission of W. W. Norton & Company, Inc.

"To White Noise" from *The Life* by Carrie Fountain, copyright © 2021 by Carrie Fountain. Used by permission of Penguin Books, an imprint of Penguin Publishing Group, a division of Penguin Random House LLC. All rights reserved.

Krista Franklin, "Extrapolating Motherhood," in *Too Much Midnight* (Haymarket Books, 2020).

Shamala Gallagher, "Final Neon," in *Late Morning When the World Burns* (The Cultural Society, 2019).

Sherine Gilmour, "Pediatric Laboratory Feces Test #1," in *So To Speak*.

Carmen Giménez Smith, "Rare Privilege," from *Cruel Futures*. Copyright © 2018 by Carmen Giménez Smith. Reprinted with the permission of The Permissions Company, LLC on behalf of City Lights Books, citylights.com.

Aracelis Girmay, excerpts from "The Black Maria," from *The Black Maria*. Copyright © 2016 by Aracelis Girmay. Reprinted with the permission of The Permissions Company, LLC on behalf of BOA Editions, Ltd., boaeditions.org.

Jenn Givhan, "The Excavation," in *The Nation*.

Camille Guthrie, "Virgil, Hey," from *Diamonds*. Originally in *The New Republic*. Copyright © 2018, 2021 by Camille Guthrie. Reprinted with the permission of The Permissions Company, LLC on behalf of BOA Editions, Ltd., boaeditions.org.

Lauren Haldeman, "I'm Your Mom," in *Bat City Review*.

Pamela Hart, "War Stories," from *Mothers over Nangarhar*. Copyright © 2019 by Pamela Hart. Reprinted with the permission of The Permissions Company, LLC on behalf of Sarabande Books, www.sarabandebooks.org.

Faylita Hicks, "The Birth Mother's Red Bath for Courage," in *HoodWitch* (Acre Books, 2019).

"When the World Was Milk" from *Milk Black Carbon* by Joan Naviyuk Kane, © 2017. Reprinted by permission of the University of Pittsburgh Press.

Keetje Kuipers, "At the Museum of Trades and Traditions," from *All Its Charms*. Copyright © 2019 by Keetje Kuipers. Reprinted with the permission of The Permissions Company, LLC on behalf of BOA Editions, Ltd., boaeditions.org.

Joy Ladin, "The Leopard." From *The Future is Trying to Tell Us Something: New and Selected Poems*. Sheep Meadow Press, 2017.

Eugenia Leigh, "Gold," in *Pleiades*.

Shara Lessley, "The Monarch," in *American Poetry Review*; "'Estranged, Changed, Suspended': My Path to Plath" in *Poetry Northwest*.

Kim-An Lieberman, "More Moon," in *In Orbit* (Blue Begonia Press, 2014).

Layli Long Soldier, ["Whereas her birth signaled . . ."], from *Whereas*. Copyright © 2017 by Layli Long Soldier. Reprinted with the permission of The Permissions Company, LLC on behalf of the author and Graywolf Press, Minneapolis, Minnesota, graywolfpress.org.

Kwoya Fagin Maples, "My Mother Bathes Me after I Give Birth," in *Mend* (University Press of Kentucky, 2018).

Joyelle McSweeney, "Sestina Gratitude," from *Toxicon and Arachne*. Copyright © 2020 by Joyelle McSweeney. Reprinted with the permission of The Permissions Company, LLC on behalf of Nightboat Books, nightboat.org.

Erika Meitner, "In Defense of the Empty Chaos Required for Adequate Preparation," from *Useful Chaos*. Originally in *The Los Angeles Review*. Copyright © 2017, 2022 by Erika Meitner. Reprinted with the permission of The Permissions Company, LLC on behalf of BOA Editions, Ltd., boaeditions.org.

Lynn Melnick, "Landscape with Clinic and Oracle," in *Landscape with Sex and Violence* (YesYes Books, 2017).

Jasminne Mendez, "Again," in *Raising Mothers*.

Clarissa Mendiola, "Nearly There," in *Storyboard: A Journal of Pacific Imagery*.

Emily Mohn-Slate, "Feed," in *The Falls* (New American Press, 2020).

Lisa L. Moore, "Raising White Men II." First appeared in *24 Hours of Men* (Dancing Girl Press, 2018).

Sara Mumolo, "10 weeks and intermittent: earning," in *Day Counter* (Omnidawn, 2018).

Aimee Nezhukumatathil, "I Could Be a Whale Shark," from *Oceanic*. Copyright © 2018 by Aimee Nezhukumatathil. Reprinted with the permission of The Permissions Company, LLC on behalf of Copper Canyon Press, coppercanyonpress.org.

January Gill O'Neil, "Maybe the Milky Way," from *Rewilding*. Copyright © 2018 by January Gill O'Neil. Reprinted with the permission of The Permissions Company, LLC on behalf of CavanKerry Press, Ltd., www.cavankerry.org.

Emmy Pérez, "Cajas/Boxes with Zero Tolerance #9," first appeared as "Cajas/Boxes of Zero Tolerance" on *The Quarry: A Social Justice Database* by Split This Rock, 2019.

Kiki Petrosino, "Confession," from *Witch Wife*. Copyright © 2017 by Kiki Petrosino. Reprinted with the permission of The Permissions Company, LLC on behalf of Sarabande Books, www.sarabandebooks.org.

Catherine Pierce, "High Dangerous," in *Danger Days* (Saturnalia, 2020) and in Academy of American Poets Poem-a-Day.

Khadijah Queen, "Mothering Solo" in *Rattle* and "Terrell Owens Private Messaged Me" in *I'm So Fine: A List of Famous Men and What I had On* (YesYes Books, 2013).

Chelsea Rathburn, "Postpartum: Lullaby," in *Still Life with Mother with Knife* (Louisiana State University Press, 2019).

Jordan Rice, "If I Admit Who I Am, Who Will Become?" first appeared as "Poetics Statement" in *Troubling the Line: Trans and Genderqueer Poetry and Poetics* (Nightboat, 2013). "Pre-Op" copyright © 2016 by Jordan Rice. Reprinted from *Constellarium* (Orison Books, 2016) by permission of Orison Books, Inc. All rights reserved. www.orisonbooks.com.

Natalie Shapero, "Monster," from *Hard Child*. Copyright © 2017 by Natalie Shapero. Reprinted with the permission of The Permissions Company, LLC on behalf of Copper Canyon Press, www.coppercanyonpress.org.

"Our Family on the Run" from *The Octopus Museum: Poems* by Brenda Shaughnessy, copyright © 2019 by Brenda Shaughnessy. Used by permission of Alfred A. Knopf, an imprint of the Knopf Doubleday Publishing Group, a division of Penguin Random House LLC. All rights reserved.

신 선 영 Sun Yung Shin, "A Series of Short Stories or Propositions," in *Under a Warm Green Linden*.

Maggie Smith, "This Year the Role of Boiling Hail Will Be Played by ________________," originally published in *McNeese Review*. © 2020 Maggie Smith.

Megan Snyder-Camp, "Baskets." A portion of this essay was first published by The Poetry Foundation, poetryfoundation.org.

Molly Spencer, "I Stop Writing the Poem: On Motherhood and the Writing Life," published in *Literary Hub* as "Against the Muse Myth: On Motherhood and the Writing Life"; "After Reading the Story of Assumption Chapel in Cold Spring, Minnesota" in *Hinge* (Southern Illinois Press, 2020). Copyright © Molly Spencer.

Melissa Stephenson, "Six Days in the Crabapple," in *Ninth Letter*, and "Confetti Time" in *Blackbird*.

Alison Stine, "The Experiment," in *The Adroit Journal*.

Angela Narciso Torres, "Nocturne," from *What Happens Is Neither*. Originally appeared as "Insomnia Poem" in *Waxwing* (Fall 2019). Copyright © 2019, 2021 by Angela Narciso Torres. Reprinted with the permission of The Permissions Company, LLC on behalf of Four Way Books, fourwaybooks.com.

Lena Khalaf Tuffaha, "The Whole Point," in *Water & Salt* (Red Hen, 2017).

Sarah Vap, "from *Winter: Aphorisms*," in *Nashville Review*.

Vanessa Angélica Villarreal "*f*= [*(root) (future)*]" in *Poetry*.

Hope Wabuke, "In This Body, You're Disappearing," in *Glass: A Journal of Poetry*.

Sasha West, "Recognition," in *The Georgia Review*.

Monica Youn, "Blackacre" from *Blackacre*. Copyright © 2016 by Monica Youn. Reprinted with the permission of The Permissions Company, LLC on behalf of Graywolf Press, Minneapolis, Minnesota, graywolfpress.org.

Rachel Zucker, "Confessional," from *SoundMachine*. Copyright © 2019 by Rachel Zucker. Reprinted with the permission of The Permissions Company, LLC on behalf of Wave Books, wavepoetry.com.

Author Index